SEMANTICS
AND COMMUNICATION

SEMANTICS AND

JOHN C. CONDON, JR.

To My Mother and Father

ACKNOWLEDGMENTS

MY FORMAL interest in the study of "language and thought" dates from the time I first took a course by that title at Northwestern University. Dean Barnlund taught the course then, but when he left to go to San Francisco State College (since reclassified), I found myself teaching it—until I also left to join the faculty at International Christian University in Tokyo. From the beginning of this interest to the present, countless colleagues and friends—most often including human beings labeled "students"—have continued to stimulate that interest. The limitations of space and, alas, memory allow my acknowledging here only a few and in no particular order. In any case, thanks to Arthur Hastings, Richard Dettering, Frank Haiman, Parke Burgess, S. I. Hayakawa, Noah Brannen, Lee Griffin, Mitsuko Saito, Edward Hall, Rae Moses, Scott Baird, Rogelio Diaz-Guerrero, Shigeko Imada, Joao Vogel . . . and my sympathetic editor at Macmillan, Lloyd Chilton. I wish also to thank my colleagues who provided suggestions for this second edition: James Gibson, William Gorden, Owen Jenson, and Beth Richmond.

J. C. C.

PREFACE TO THE
SECOND EDITION

A LOT has happened in the ten years since the first edition of this book was written. A semantic history of the past decade might actually reveal changes in our society and ways of talking and thinking more clearly than almost any other kind of history. In re-reading the first edition, I find that a word like *Negro* stands out as archaic, though civil rights leaders were discussing the semantics of race even then and some argued that changing *Negro* to *Black* was only semantic, and wouldn't change anything. Women, or some women anyway, later came to demand semantic changes, too: the decade gave us *Ms.*, *chairperson*, and *sexism*. It may be another decade before we can judge the impact of such changes, though we will speculate on that in this edition. The hippies came on strong, along with a whole hip vocabulary and symbol system, so beatniks went the way of Bohemians. Drug slang and Black slang came into the establishment idiom, and even some old Rotarians came to say "right on!" Freedom to say or print in public things that were never permitted in the past shook up many people who liked the distinction between "clean words" and "dirty words." Wheaties stopped being "the breakfast of champions" as Ralph Nader—like the ghost of Alfred

Korzybski—fought for better maps in advertisingland. Latin left the Roman Catholic Mass at the same time that Eugene McCarthy said it went over into Pentagon reports.

Surely it was the Vietnam War, and later Watergate, that most influenced the semantics of the past decade. Either would have been sufficient to lead to a massive distrust of words: the "strategic hamlets" that might better have been labeled "concentration camps"; the napalm that came out sounding like something mother used to make—"incindergel"; the Latinate labels like "pacification" that had nothing to do with peace; the body counts, the "light at the end of the tunnel," the overnight change from the "Vietnam War" to the "Indo-China War," the village that had to be destroyed in order to save it, the "peace with honor." A generation freaked out. Ten years ago some students were concerned about standards for distinguishing among facts, inferences, judgments, and tautologies, but that concern began to seem futile for some of the brighter students because it was all just words. And worse, it pretended to be rational, but rationality, they said, gave us computerized bombing and body counts. So horoscopes came in—and Tarot cards, I Ching, nonverbal relating, sensitivity training, and other forms of communication that seemed outside the grasp of words.

Then came Watergate, and suddenly people were again beginning to discriminate in their use of words. Reporters shouted back when the President's Press Secretary excused his false reports by saying they were "inoperative." Suddenly it was clear that if some words did not match facts or if some labels were grossly misleading they could not be dismissed as problems of "mere semantics." Jail was a reality. And the public concern was not limited to any group that could be dismissed with a label, like "hippies" or "radicals."

Korzybski embarked on his philosophy of symbolism, his general semantics, at the end of World War I, in the midst of the disillusionment over that "war to end all wars," that "war to make the word safe for democracy." In his time there were artists like the dadaists, not so different in some respects from some of the yippies, who responded with their own forms of the put-down of lofty symbols a half century later. But Korzybski, John

Dewey, and a great number of philosophers of that time, who might have little else in common, tried to set higher standards for the ways in which we use words and to prevent some of the ways words have used us. They urged a new beginning.

What will happen in the next ten years? Semantically, we might not be able to take another decade like the past one. And yet as I write this, I realize that the examples cited here and maybe "the point," too, will soon seem as if they came from another era, just as references to John Profumo in the first edition surely do now. Where have you gone, Mrs. Robinson? Where have you gone, John Profumo? Out of print, out of mind. The best semantics text is still today's newspaper —available in paperback.

JOHN C. CONDON, JR.

Communication Department
Language Division
International Christian University
Tokyo

CONTENTS

THREE

FOUR

FIVE

ONE
INTRODUCTION
TO AN ATTITUDE

It is conventional to begin a textbook with a brief definition of its subject matter. A book on semantics, however, might begin by asking the reader what *semantics* means. This is not a rhetorical question. Nor is the author being coy or pleading ignorance. If you, the reader, answer the question honestly, you are already on your way to understanding what this book is all about.

Suppose, for example, that you are taking a course in semantics or one that talks about semantics. Then your response might be something like this: "*Semantics* is the word used by people who can't agree on anything and so they agree they are having problems with semantics." Or: "*Semantics* is a word in the course where we talk about words." Or even: "*Semantics* is the name of the course where that cute blond sits next to me." All of these responses are relevant to the question (though they may not be acceptable for some instructors' examinations—so you should be careful what you underline in this book) because all are possible responses to the word *semantics*. And the study of semantics is the study of how persons respond to words and other symbols.

Now, perhaps you have just underlined the previous sentence, in which case *semantics* means, in part, that particular response. By the time you complete the book, with several yards of underlined (literally or mentally) phrases, the subject will have come to produce some change in attitude, be it to boredom or ecstasy (hopefully neither). The subject here is not so much a catalog of definitions and observations as it is an attitude toward language, reality, and human behavior. And this is another reason why it is unwise to begin the book with a concise definition: to do so would be to miss the point. To paraphrase for our purposes what somebody once replied when asked, "What is Zen Buddhism?"—first of all, it is not answering a question like that!

We might do better to indicate what the subject is *not*, because the word *semantics* is used in many ways in conversation and can be confusing. Like its older cousin, *rhetoric*, the word *semantics* is often used pejoratively, referring to verbal nuances or hair-splitting distinctions. "Look, let's not get hung up on semantics"; or, "It was nothing, only a semantic problem"; such remarks are not uncommon. But, as we shall see shortly, calling something "a mere semantic problem" is itself another kind of semantic problem: that label "mere semantic problem" often means, in effect, "trivial problem," or "irrelevant," etc., and hence one that might be ignored. Obviously, the kinds of "semantic problems" in which we will be interested are not best regarded as trivial, irrelevant, or *mere*.

The term *semantics* is used more seriously to identify "the study of meanings." [1] And yet there are many approaches to "meaning," not all of which are relevant to our interests. Some scholars trace the historical development of words (etymology or philosophy); some other scholars in linguistics study the diffusion or spread of words over a social and geographical area, noting regional differences. Such studies are often quite interesting and informative, even

---

[1] Usually, this refers to the study of meanings of *words*, and less often the meanings of other conventional symbols (religious symbols, coats-of-arms, flags, etc.). There are also special names for each of these studies, however. In recent years the semantics of nonverbal expressions has attracted greater interest. Because of the limitations of the scope of this book, however, our concern will be primarily with the verbal level, usually within the range of single words to phrases, not smaller units such as phonemes or larger units such as essays, speeches, or novels.

helpful—so long as one does not conclude from such studies what a word *should* mean.

Semantics and Semiotics

Years ago, Charles Morris proposed a new discipline that would be a general study of symbolic behavior which he called *semiotics*.[2] He divided the subject matter into three parts. One of these he called *semantics*, or the study of the relationship between words (and other symbols) and what these words represent. For example, the word "book" represents the thing you are looking at. A second part of semiotics was *syntactics*, or the study of the relationship between words and other words, symbols and other symbols. Syntactics thus includes grammar, syntax, logic—in short, all rules of symbol systems, the rules that make "This is a book." one kind of statement, "Is this a book?" another kind, and "a this book is" a garbled sentence at best. The third part of his division he called *pragmatics*, the study of the relationships between words (and other symbols) and human behavior, including the way words and other symbols influence how we act. Today "semantics" is popularly used to mean more or less what Morris described, the study of symbols and their referents. But that is not exactly what *this* book is all about.

Our interest leads us to a more *general* semantics, one that does not look only at words and things but at the human behavior that results from using symbols in particular ways. In terms of Morris' definition of semiotics, we are equally concerned with the pragmatic as well as the semantic aspect of symbols. Indeed, we may argue that one cannot tell the meaning of most words without observing how the word is used, and what effect it seems to have on our behavior.

This makes our interest considerably different from that of most linguists, who usually are content to examine the syntactic dimension of languages, language as a system unto itself. And until very recently, most linguists were reluctant to approach even the nar-

---

[2] Charles Morris, *Signs, Language and Behavior*. Englewood Cliffs, N.J.: Prentice-Hall, 1946.

rower view of semantics, for such a study naturally took them outside of the system to the world of "reality." Perhaps the closest most linguists have come to this interest is in hybrid disciplines such as socio-linguistics, ethno-linguistics, or psycho-linguistics.

Count Alfred Korzybski (1877–1950) who coined the term *general semantics* was himself as much concerned with psychology as with "mere words." Korzybski believed that language influenced not only our thinking, but all of human behavior. The effect, he felt, was part of our nervous systems. Thus, if our language habits were immature or distorted, our behavior would also be less than mature. Indeed, most of human behavior, from Korzybski's point of view, was "unsane." He sought to achieve a universal therapy through the linguistic retraining of human nervous systems. The title of his major work, *Science and Sanity*,[3] states his concern rather clearly. (Unfortunately, the rest of the book is not so clear.)

Some day behavioral semantics may pass into another field, perhaps psycho-linguistics, perhaps semiotics, perhaps some as yet undeveloped discipline that will fully incorporate studies of nonverbal languages—music, film, art, or whatever—with the traditional concern with words. In the meantime, semantics takes its place among the behavioral sciences as an approach leading to an attitude about what makes us behave as we do, be it wisely or foolishly, sanely or "unsanely."

It is during college, perhaps for the first time, that we become self-conscious about language and communication, and hence with semantics. As a student you may feel that you are now among an elite of the curious and intelligent, qualities that are both verbally based. From the library to the dorm, yours is very much a world of words. You take seriously some of the noises made by the professor or by your roommate (and more seriously, still, the sound of your own voice). You agonize over scratches on paper, called themes or term projects or examinations, and you submit them knowing they will return with still more scratches—which you may take still more seriously.

You explore the world with pen and book, and you carry home

---

[3] *Science and Sanity*, Second Edition (Lakeville, Conn.: The International Non-Aristotelian Library, 1947).

verbal treasures. You apprentice yourself to new verbal skills. You attempt new verbal strategies. Instead of calling your parents "old fashioned and stingy," you may accuse them of "pursuing the Protestant ethic." Instead of calling your girl friend or boy friend "a poor sport," you explain all about "defense mechanisms, anxiety, and neurosis." You abandon sleep in favor of questions—questions like "What is Truth?" or "What is God?" or "Are people *really* good?" You discuss until you are bored or amused by the answers or lack of them, but you discuss. You formulate an answer but it does not sound quite as profound as the answer by Plato or Kierkegaard. You comfort yourself by knowing that you are in good company. In your waking life, and even during some of your sleep, the verbal activity is constant.

This book is written with the modest hope that if you can understand your language habits and communication processes a little better, all this verbal activity may be a little more significant.

Our Symbol-Laden Culture

Millions of Americans begin their day something like this: A radio alarm clock awakens them, perhaps with music, and later with news. They dress according to the fashion and what the weather report recommends; they listen to the news of prison riots, of wars in far-off lands, or sports scores from across the nation. A famous man has died, and the millions are saddened, if only briefly. They may gobble down a vitamin pill but then skip breakfast, quickly brush their teeth, and hurry off to work. If they drive, they watch their speedometer to stay under the legal limit while keeping track of how much time they still have to arrive at their destination on time. This is how the day begins.

For a day to commence (and continue) in this manner these millions must have accepted a very sophisticated and complex set of symbols, for there is very little in the description that is not heavily endowed with symbols. The *clock* that wakes one—a revolutionary change from not so many centuries ago, when the sunrise or a rooster did the job with the result that days varied considerably from season to season. With the invention of the clock, the abstract notion of time was arbitrarily marked off into convenient units. The *clothing*—a choice of formal or casual, of coat and tie for men, of heels for women; how many buttons on the coat, how wide the tie, how high the heels, all of these arbitrary decisions are quite unrelated to the more practical purpose of keeping the body comfortable. This is not to say that style means nothing to these millions, for the hyperbolic woman "would rather *die* than be caught in last year's style!" The *news reports* that enrage or sadden them are of people they have never met, of events they can never know, of places they have never been. Nevertheless, for these millions the names on the news "mean" more than the names of their neighbors. The *vitamin pill* appears to be like thousands of other pills, but the label on the bottle is impressive with its fine print of unpronounceable names. And besides, anything that costs that much must have *something*. They compulsively brush their teeth, because they believe that brushing prevents cavities (though most do not really know why). Their wallets and purses are filled with other symbols: money, credit cards, licenses, and identification cards without which, in a symbol-laden culture, they may be unable to prove who they are. They drive on the right side of the street because they agreed to do so. They agree to travel at a speed that traffic signs permit and assume that their speed is correct when a needle on the dashboard points to the appropriate number. And the millions hurry to their destinations because they have agreed to begin work at nine, and being too early will communicate something undesirable to their colleagues (and themselves, perhaps) and being too late will communicate something else to their bosses. Out of respect for the millions, we will end the story before the day's *work* begins.

The history of human civilization is a history of the increasing importance of the symbolic dimension of life. By and large, increased industrialization brings with it increased systems of symbols. We have to learn many languages we do not even recognize as such; man lives not by words alone. Susanne Langer has said that "the symbol-making function is one of man's primary activities, like eating, looking, or moving about."[4] We might add that our symbols

[4] Susanne Langer, *Philosophy in a New Key* (Cambridge: Harvard University Press, 1942), p. 41.

pervade even those activities: what, when, and how much we eat; what we see and do not see; and how and where we move about are themselves bound up in symbols. In Japan, *sashimi* and *nori* are delicious; in translation, "raw fish" and "sea-weed" sound awful to many people who have never tried them, mainly because of our symbolic associations of what is edible and what is not.

Of all of the symbol systems, the language of words is by far the most important. It is essential that we examine more closely these symbols we live by.

Of Mice and Men, Signs and Symbols

There are many metaphors for what language is for man. It is a tool, a map, a weapon, a toy, a surrogate, a mask—many metaphors for the many functions of language. All of the functions of language, if they are to aid man, in some ways affect that most basic need of any living organism, survival. From the premise that survival is desirable, it follows that the language that best aids survival is the best language. The implication of this conclusion is the subject of most of this chapter.

Darwin's thesis holds for man as well as for any animal: that when the survival mechanism of any creature fails, that animal ceases to exist. What the bee or the beaver needed to survive in 1676 is the same mechanism the bee or beaver employs in 1976. And if conditions should change greatly in those three hundred years, the bee and beaver will join the brontosaurus. The skill for survival is built into the animals, a literal and complete "design for living." Adopt another skill as occasion demands, the animal cannot.

But man is something different. Man has developed a physiology slightly different from his nearest simian brother. Man possesses a forebrain (cortex) larger than the "closest ape," and this distinction, which is one of degree, permits a behavior that is utterly different in kind. With his enlarged forebrain man can perform an exercise more marvelous than any of the animals he sometimes praises: man is able to think. And, as W. Grey Walter[5] puts it, physiologically

[5] W. Grey Walter, *The Living Brain* (New York: W. W. Norton, 1953), p. 15.

speaking, *Cogito ergo sum* is true for man; man exists (survives) because he can think.

> Man . . . is specifically what he is by virtue of thought, and owes his survival in the struggle for existence to the development of that supreme function of the brain. He is sapiens, the thinking species of the genus homo. The discerning, discreet and judicious one, even if he does not always live up to all these meanings of the name he has given himself.

Because no animal possesses the more fully developed forebrain that makes language possible, the communication skills of an animal are rather limited. In nature, animals have many ingenious (to us) ways of warning of danger or of flirting with a mate or of passing on useful information. Bees give directions to each other by dancing. Porpoises seem to have a small vocabulary of meaningful noises that they burble at each other. In captivity, animals can be taught some new skills: parrots are accustomed to saying a few words in public, and even old dogs can learn a few new tricks. The young ape can be taught to outperform the human infant. One ape has been taught to mouthe a half-dozen words. Recently, too, some chimpanzees have learned to perform simple arithmetic exercises, using a machine constructed for this purpose. But only the lowest level of what could be called a "verbal skill" can be learned by any creature besides man.

Animals, of course, communicate with each other. Research into animal languages is now calling into question some of the earlier notions about why man was so different from other animals. Still it seems clear that man's use of symbols, including what is usually called "imagination" is beyond even the brightest ape. A rat may learn to find its way through a maze by trial and error, but it cannot plan the trip by studying a map.

In terms of survival, man's ability to think means many things. It means, first of all, that man can adapt himself to new or changing conditions. It took Noah to build the ark, for even if the animals could sense the storm, they could not call themselves together to weather it out. The ability to think means also that man gives himself skills he was not born with. It is true that man was not made to fly, but in two generations he has become the most skillful flier known. The ability to think means that to a great extent man can create the kind of environment he wants to live in; only man can now live comfortably at any point on the earth, or under the seas or even away from the earth.

Unfortunately, along with the marvelous achievements of man come blunders and stupidity and cruelty that are unknown even to a rat. For though man can turn the desert into a garden, can plan his community, his birthrate, and increase his lifespan, only man can also plan his death or the death of his entire species. And no white rat would flee his property because a black rat had moved into the hole next door.

The ability to use language means the ability to transfer something of experience into symbols and *through the symbolic medium to share experience*. Man, through his ability to use language, is capable of learning from the past. Man has thus advanced while other creatures have not, cannot. Because man's experience is built upon experience, change accelerates at a geometric rate. Witness the developments in the past fifty years as compared to the previous fifteen hundred. As we enter the "Age of the Computer," the promises for man are almost incredible. Never before has the retrieval and analysis of information been possible with the speed or accuracy permitted by this cybernetic revolution. To transfer the symbolic experience into meaningful human behavior is, of course, another task, a task that, up until now, man has not always taken onto himself.

To briefly review, man is distinguished physiologically from animals by an enlarged forebrain or cortex that makes language and thought possible. Through language man can express his experience in symbols, and through those symbols he can share his experiences with his fellow man. The sharing of meaningful experiences results in the change we call learning. As man learns he advances, or at least changes, from generation to generation. Animals, which are capable of communicating in varied but comparatively limited ways, cannot learn from each other, cannot change, cannot advance, at least not to the extent that man does.

The distinction between man and animals finds its counterpart in the kinds of communication performed by each. Animals can learn to respond to signs, but it seems that only man can use symbols effectively. Susanne Langer expresses the difference by saying that signs announce but symbols remind. That is, animals can emit and receive cries signifying food or sex or danger. But an animal cannot contemplate the nature of food and thereby decide it might be a good idea to go on a diet.

One distinction between sign and symbol is the difference in the number of possible responses to each. A sign stands in a one-to-one relationship to an experience (or object or the like); a symbol suggests many possible responses. A sign of danger, such as a loud noise, may only stimulate an animal to flee or hide. But the symbol of danger to man may mean many things, of which fleeing might be the least useful. It is easy to think of signs which man has devised, but it is difficult to find them used only as signs. Take, for example, the loud noise of a car honking. In some situations the honking may mean "get out of the way"—but it probably is more symbolic than that. The person honked at may have to consider if the driver is indicating "get out of my way," "hello, it's me," "happy wedding day" or even "impeach the President." Man-devised signs tend to become symbolic; for animals, responses are more restricted, and a sign remains a sign. The variety of responses with which man may respond to symbols gives him increased flexibility and requires him to pause for consideration of the most appropriate responses before acting. To jump at every warning is to put man at the level of the rabbit.

Mark Twain[6] once made this same observation when he noted that we sometimes behave like animals instead of behaving like people:

> We should be careful to get out of an experience only the wisdom that is in it—and stop there; lest we be like the cat that sits down on a hot stove lid. She will never sit down on a hot stove-lid again, and that is well; but also she will never sit down on a cold one anymore.

To go from cat to mouse, we may recall Wendell Johnson's remark on this distinction: "To a mouse, cheese is cheese; that's why mousetraps work."

The more restrictive a society is, perhaps, the greater the em-

[6] Bernard DeVoto (ed.), *The Portable Mark Twain* (New York: Viking, 1946), p. 563.

phasis on signs. The military, for example, may impose rigid standards for behavior that some would call *signal reactions*. (If it moves, salute it.) Also in times of stress, man often responds to a word (symbol) as if it were a sign: he reacts signally. As he does so he acts more like an animal than a human being.

Man creates a few signs for his immediate reactions. The alarm-clock buzzer, the class bell, and the stop sign are each designed by man to elicit one appropriate and immediate response. But such signs are few. Inappropriate signal reactions are, unfortunately, more common. Whether we jump to conclusions, refuse to listen to information because of a label we have given its source ("don't believe anything *she* says"), or blush at certain words, we are also responding signally. Such reactions fail to use the resources of language as they might best be used. Learning to use language intelligently begins by learning not to be used by language.

Symbolic Transformation

Our interest in semantics begins with the realization that our symbolic behavior, including our speaking habits, *transform a given "reality" into many symbolic realities*. Richard Dettering pointed out that if you bring a cat and a dog together, the cat may cringe or run in reaction to that dog. The way to remove the danger is to remove the dog (or the cat). But put a child with that same dog and you have another possibility. At first the child may react in ways not so different from those of the cat, and you still may have to remove the dog (or the child). But you may also *remove the threat symbolically:* "Nice doggy, it likes you," and so on.

It would be helpful if we could go back to reality, back to the time described in Genesis where God had created the world and left it up to Adam to name the things around him. If we could do that, we could start with "reality" and compare to it the symbols that we have come to apply to that reality. Unfortunately, as we will discuss in the next chapter, the reality around us is already transformed symbolically. We've lost that innocence of Eden, too. So it will be difficult for us to talk about the simpler semantics of "words" and "things," for even the "things" are endowed with symbolism.

TWO
FROM EXPERIENCE
TO SYMBOL

Like anything else of value, language is best used when it is best understood. When misunderstood, language habits can lead to behavior that is at best foolish and at worst tragic.

A First Assumption: Tentative

A common misunderstanding is the assumption that language is neutral, a medium of exchange between the world and man that in no way affects man's behavior. Such an assumption presents language as a process as natural as breathing, something not to be examined very carefully and certainly not to be altered in any but the most superficial ways, such as by increasing a vocabulary or improving pronunciation. When one takes his language for granted, he may logically conclude that everybody else in the world thinks very much as he does, means what he means when he uses a word. Or, if they do not, then the others must be somehow confused, uneducated, peculiar, or simply wrong.

A more sophisticated approach to language—and this is what semantics is all about—can afford to assume very little. The assumption with which we begin this chapter may appear to be eminently sensible, even obvious. But by the conclusion of the chapter we will have reason to modify it as well.

We begin, tentatively, with the assumption that whatever words might be considered, they are definitely something very different from the things they represent. Semantics usually begins with that assumption of duality. The distinction has usually been stated in the negative: "the word is not the thing." Linguists and psycholinguists are developing descriptions of the nature of "words," whereas the philosophers originally and the scientists currently have pursued the investigation of "things." Studying the relationship between the two and emphasizing the importance of the distinction is the special province of the semanticists.

Sensible critics (including, perhaps, you) often have been puzzled by a discipline that emphasizes what appears to be so obvious. Who, after all, would assume that "a word" was the "the thing" it symbolizes? The answer, semanticists reply, is written throughout history and through much of our daily lives, in which we seek after, purchase, love, fight, and sometimes die for "words." As our culture becomes more symbol laden, even symbol bound, the recognition of that distinction becomes still more important.

The ability to symbolize means the ability to call up internal experiences, using only the symbols. Whether one is reading a novel or reading a grade on some term paper, the symbols stimulate some changes in the body chemistry. For example, if before retiring to bed, you read a ghost story, you may find it difficult to fall asleep immediately. You are not *really* afraid of ghosts, but your reactions to little marks on paper may affect your behavior in a way you cannot control. Or, if before retiring to bed, you read a textbook, you may find it difficult to stay awake. (Here, of course, we are not talking about the relative merits of ghosts and academics, but about one's attitude toward such symbols.) Or, to take one more common example from the classroom, you might consider the power of your instructor to affect your nervous system just by organizing three lines to form either an A or an F. What has caused the changes are clearly responses to "symbols"; such responses are sometimes called *semantic reactions*. For more dramatic examples, you might read the literature of psychosomatic medicine or note the power of "suggestion" that a hypnotist can exert on a subject.

Thus the semanticist is interested not only in "words" as different from "things" but even more in the pervasive responses to symbols as opposed to possible reactions to something in the nonverbal world.

The World As Perceived

If you have ever flown in a plane, this recollection may be familiar to you: From the window you see below a landscape clear and ordered. Along the coast line, the waves press methodically. You can almost see their birth from a silent sea and their steady movement to the shore where they disappear. Each wave is separate. You can count them. Inland the pattern of traffic moves slowly, without noise, without confusion. There a bus moves out to pass a truck; there the cars slow at what must be a stoplight. The back yards of the houses are clearly marked, and in the distance the patches of farmland neatly mark their own borders.

The view is a pleasant one, but since you spend most of your time on the ground, you know that neither shoreline nor terrain is so ordered and so without movement and clash. You know that as your plane descends the world seems to speed up, the invisible becomes immediate, the silent becomes noise, and the few become innumerable. What had been a patch of green becomes a park of trees with shimmering leaves. What had been a steady glow of orange becomes a sputtering neon sign.

When your feet are firmly on the ground you must realize that you have not returned from illusion to reality. You have only returned to what is most familiar. If you had the proper apparatus you could descend still farther into a microscopic world as apparently different from the familiar landscape as it had seemed when viewed from the plane.

The history of physics has been the history of this kind of descent into the stuff of the world, always seeking that ultimate level beyond which there is no further change. As the exploration of the submicroscopic world progressed, physicists were forced to abandon what previous generations had thought was permanent: elements, then atoms, later electrons and protons, once believed to be the indestructible stuff of the world, successively failed the tests of permanence. Where has this exploration brought us today? And what does this have to do with semantics? Bertrand Russell[1] describes both:

> Energy had to replace matter as what is permanent. But energy, unlike matter, is not a refinement of the common-sense notion of a "thing"; it is merely *a characteristic of physical processes*. *(Italics added.)*

What characterizes "reality" at all levels is not the presence of some "thing," but rather of a process. Rather than speak of the *things* of the world we should speak of the *events*.

Our language is a product of centuries, and most of our vocabulary reflects an older, prescientific view of the world. We retain a vocabulary suggestive of permanence when we know today that the only permanence *is* change. Metaphorically, we speak of "the *things* of the world" as if they were like rocks, when we know they are more like flames. What we once thought were "like nouns" now seem more "like verbs." In the light of the discoveries of the past century, our vocabulary is peculiarly anachronistic. Of course we need not, and certainly cannot change our language. But being aware that a nonverbal world of *process* is represented in words that indicate a *static* quality is important.

In one sense the essential awareness in the study of semantics is the awareness of what we cannot directly perceive, that world-in-flux. This is fundamental in the assumption that no words can ever accurately represent "a thing," for "things" are dynamic and words are static. Of equal importance in a discussion of the "things" of the world is the awareness of the process by which we apprehend the events of reality, perception. For just as there is much we are incapable of perceiving, there is much that we can perceive but characteristically do not.

The human perceptual apparatus is impressive, even if it cannot notice the continuous process in the world. Unaided, the eye can discriminate among an estimated seven million colors. It can see an object the size of a grapefruit at a distance of a quarter mile. But the

---

[1] Bertrand Russell, A *History of Western Philosophy* (New York: Simon and Schuster, 1945), p. 47.

perceptual apparatus is also confusing. It fools us into thinking that the moon grows smaller as it "rises" in the sky (and is actually closer). When still pictures are flashed at the speed of sixteen per second, we see the pleasant illusion of a continuous natural motion of the screen. It may be said that everything we see is an "optical illusion" that is the result of our training, values, and goals. Like the familiar optical illusions that appear in children's magic books and Sunday newspaper supplements, what we see depends on how we look at "it" and who is doing the looking.

What we see (or hear, smell, feel, and so on) depends on what we think we want and need to see. And this in turn depends on who and and where we have been and who we think we will become. Perception is an active process, not something "natural" or identical for all persons with comparable eyesight. The human being seems to need to be selective of all of the possible stimuli. We need to organize the stimuli, to disregard the apparently irrelevant (and sometimes the threatening), and to "make sense" out of the stimuli we do perceive. If we were sensitive to the billions of stimuli that bombard us each second, we would be rendered incapable of doing anything. (Pause from your reading for a second and look carefully at this page—see all of the tiny pits and marks on the paper that you had not noticed; perhaps you can observe delicate shadings in the paper of colors you had not seen before, colors that are especially difficult to distinguish verbally. Now listen carefully for sounds you had not noticed before.) If the unfunctional marks on the paper or the irrelevant sounds were important to us, we could learn to perceive them—but we could not notice all of the marks and still concentrate on reading the page, or hear all of the sounds in the air and still follow a serious conversation. We must be aware that we are constantly being selective, and that what we do perceive is but the tiniest part of what is perceptible.

Gestalt psychologists have studied why we perceive as we do, emphasizing the need to organize the stimuli that "meet the eye" (and other sensory organs). We think we see the details of a familiar face in a newspaper photograph, but on closer examination we can see that there are only tiny dots, regularly spaced but of various sizes, which produce the apparent blacks, whites, and shades of grey. There is no "face" on the page; there are only stimuli that *we can organize* into a face. We *create* what we see around us in a way not so different from the summer entertainment of making animals out of cloud shapes (or clouds out of animal shapes, for that matter).

We see mostly what we have learned to look at. We look at what we think we *need* to look at. We ignore what seems unnecessary or, in some cases, what seems threatening. However, we are *sensitive* to far more stimuli than we may realize.

An experiment was conducted in which pictures were flashed on a screen at such a rate that those watching could not be sure what they were seeing. Instruments were set up to record eye movements during the process. Even though the subjects in the experiment were not consciously aware of what they were seeing, the pupils of their eyes contracted when the pictures were distasteful or threatening. "Neutral pictures" produced no such responses.[2] The point would be missed if we thought this perceptual phenomenon occurs only in the psychological laboratory. Such unconscious avoidance of personal "danger" is a part of our everyday behavior.

A similar experiment testing one's ability to recognize words flashed on the screen for a very short time indicated that individuals characteristically "see" words that are consistent with their personal values and misread words that are irrelevant or opposed to their value systems. For example, one subject who had ranked low in the "aesthetic" area of a standard value test misread the word *elegant* as *hyprocrisy*.[3]

One's culture as well as one's personal background also influences perception. In another experiment, people from the United States and from Mexico viewed pairs of pictures through a stereopticon of the sort usually used to create the illusion of three-dimensionality. In this case, however, the two pictures were completely different. One represented a scene from Mexico (a bull fight, for example), the other a scene from the United States (a baseball game, for example). Several sets were shown to both groups. Con-

[2] Eckhard H. Hess and James Polt, "Pupil Size as Related to Interest Value of Visual Stimuli," *Science*, **132** (1960), pp. 349–350.

[3] Leo Postman, Jerome S. Bruner, and Elliott McGinnies, "Personal Values As Selective Factors in Perception," *Journal of Abnormal and Social Psychology* **43** (April, 1948), pp. 142–154.

sistently the North Americans "saw" the American scenes, the Mexicans "saw" only the Mexican scenes.

If you have traveled in another country whose language you did not know, perhaps the signs you noticed most were the ubiquitous ads for Coca-Cola or other familiar products. Such ads do not really dominate the landscape of the world, but when we are given the set to see them they often seem to. We see what we have learned to see. We tend to "listen" more closely to songs we have heard before than to new melodies. We pay more attention to what is pleasing to us than to the unpleasant. We tend to listen more carefully to a football game we are winning than one we are losing. We tend to prefer to hear the political candidates we favor and to read the magazines that reassure us of our social perceptions rather than those that show us "another picture."

The effect of memory and expectations based on past experience is so strong that we frequently "see" things that are not really there and fail to see things that are there. Read the phrase in the triangle below:

If you did not find an error, read it again and ask yourself why you did not see it. The explanation for this is the same explanation for the inability of some parents to notice their children growing up, or for some professors to see a bias in their reasoning; and for most of us to see inconsistencies in our behavior.

This myopia increases when we are under stress or in conflict. Psychologists Albert Hastorf and Hadley Cantril[4] have written a provocative (and yet familiar) description of what happens when the students and alumni of rival colleges watch a football game. Their investigation showed the extent to which apparently sane, educated

[4] Albert H. Hastorf and Hadley Cantril, "They Saw a Game: A Case Study," *Journal of Abnormal and Social Psychology* 49 (January, 1954), pp. 129–134.

men and women are unable to agree on what has happened, even after the cheering has stopped and the event is viewed on film. Princeton fans "saw" dirty playing on the part of Dartmouth, with refereeing that was patently unfair. Dartmouth fans "saw" the same improper conduct, but to them it was obviously the fault of the Princeton eleven. Their analysis of a Dartmouth-Princeton football game lead the investigators to a conclusion about perception that applies to all events. It is a conclusion, we might add, that is at the foundation of the semantic attitude:

> . . . It is inaccurate and misleading to say that different people have different "attitudes" concerning the same "thing." For the "thing" simply is *not* the same for different people whether the "thing" is a football game, a presidential candidate, Communism, or spinach. We do not simply "react to" a happening or to some impingement from the environment in a determined way (except in behavior that has become reflexive or habitual). We behave according to what we bring to the occasion, and what each of us brings to the occasion is more or less unique. And except for these significances which we bring to the occasion, the happenings around us would be meaningless occurrences, would be "inconsequential."[5]

A man trained in any profession or skill learns to see, to hear, to "sense," what the unskilled cannot. Learning almost anything requires a change in sensitivity. As people are of different occupations and possess different skills and interests, perceptions vary accordingly. Even in areas where no special training is required, what one sees and what one is blind to depends on his interest and background.

The young mother learns to hear the sound of her baby crying, although visitors to her home hear nothing. From the subtlest clues, one can perceive if something is troubling a close friend or mate.

Without training we may not be aware that we are not perceiving what the trained person perceives. In learning a foreign language, for example, careful training is necessary even to *hear*, not to mention imitate, new sounds. To the Spanish speaker who is learn-

[5] Ibid., p. 133.

ing English, our *yes* and his "zhess" sound alike, just as when we learn Spanish his *mesa* and our "maysuh" sound alike to us.

What all of these comments mean is that not only do we fail to see what is "out there" with anything resembling "ideal objectivity," but we constantly rehearse our own peculiar perceptions. We enjoy becoming experts at being ourselves. And as we gather with like-minded (not to say right-minded) individuals, we give ourselves support that the way we look at the world must be correct—for, after all, everybody else we know and respect sees pretty much the same thing. Our perceptions are most clearly limited and guided when the reality is social, when we look at the political, racial, economic, moral pictures. Ask yourself how many friends you have who see a world different from yours. Ask yourself what books or magazines you read that show a world different from what you like to believe exists. In the broadest sense, "perception" of the world has less to do with the sensory organs of the physical body than it does with the social body.

Abstracting

General semanticists have used the word *abstract* as an active verb to describe the process of perception. Abstracting involves three related phenomena: *ignoring* much of the stimuli that might be perceived; *focusing* on a limited amount of that stimuli; and, often *combining or rearranging* what is perceived to fit into some pattern that is particularly meaningful to the perceiver. These same three aspects of perception also characterize other aspects of our behavior. When we try to remember something, for example, we usually can recall only a small portion of what we had known or experienced; most is forgotten, we give special emphasis to only a small part of what we experienced, and part of what we recall is likely to be a rearrangement of what was originally perceived as separate. Also, when we pass along information to another person, some loss and some distortion is almost inevitable, following the same pattern just described. All that we can know is known through this active process. And all that we know is therefore a distortion of what "is really there." This should not cause alarm when you think about it. But if you think about it, it should encourage a more cautious, less dogmatic attitude about "your knowledge." For surely, of those two words, the emphasis should be on the adjective and not the noun.

The simple notion of abstracting is extremely important. For one thing, it suggests that we will have trouble comparing words or other symbols with some objective "reality." *"Reality" is, practically, what we have already abstracted.* Edmund Leach, a leading British cultural anthropologist, makes a similar point in speaking of man's relationship to his culture:[6]

> Travellers have often remarked of Australian aborigines that they seem to "read the desert like a book," and this is a very literal truth. Such knowledge is not carried in any man's head, it is in the environment. The environment is not a natural thing; it is a set of interrelated percepts, a product of culture. It yields food to the aborigine but none to the white traveller because the former perceives food where the latter sees only inedible insects.

> The bewilderment of many "ordinary" men in the environment of modern science is very similar. The environment is meaningless because we do not understand the code which would give perceptual order to our mechanical desert.

In school one of the most obvious procedures of abstracting is taking notes in a classroom. It must be very uncommon for any two students to take exactly the same notes of what was said. Sitting in different parts of the classroom probably has some influence on what is heard in the first place, and different guesses about what might be asked on an examination and different attitudes about exams also will have an effect. Personal fatigue, interest in the subject, familiarity with the teacher's methods of lecturing, and much more come into play. The teacher says that "Although you won't be tested on this you should know something about Aristotle: that he was born in 384 B.C. in the little town of Stagira on the eastern coast of the peninsula of Chalcidice in Thrace, the son of a

[6] Edmund Leach, "Culture and Social Cohension: An Anthropologist's View," in Gerald Holton (ed.), *Science and Culture* (Boston: Beacon Press, 1967), 24–38.

court physician, Nicomachus." One student writes: "*Aristotle: born 384 B.C.*" Another writes: "*Aristotle born on stagnant coast—son of a Greek physicist.*" Another writes: "*See if Marge is free tonight.*"

Because we must abstract and organize only certain stimuli, it seems impossible to "accurately" represent the world in symbolic terms. We can become conscious of our abstracting, but being aware of our limitations is quite different from overcoming them. Perhaps it is this awareness of possibilities and limitations that best describes what we call "an education." It is an awareness, at least, that is basic to a study of semantics. Without it we might repeat the error characteristic of much of Western thought—to accept an *a priori* reality and set about to name the parts of "it." Our assumption is that there is no "it"; that there are as many "it"s as there are people at any given moment in history.

A Second Look at That First Assumption

The distinction between the nonverbal (world of "things," "events," and so on) and the verbal, the object and its symbol, was the starting point for this brief examination of semantics. One cannot pursue the distinction very long before he runs into the problem of expressing "the thing," the nonverbal world, without the aid of language. In a book or lecture, of course, to designate any aspect of the nonverbal world requires a word, but the problem is not reduced when one does not speak or write but merely "experiences things" or points at things. For as soon as one begins to experience what he calls "heat" or "pain" or "light," he must ask himself whether he has not already arbitrarily (through symbols) abstracted some experience he might call "heat" or "pain" or "light." Can we ever perceive "anything" without the influence of language by which we separate "any*thing*" from "some*thing* else"?

One "commonsense" view says, "of course we can view things apart from what we call them. Things are things, and words are only applied later. So whether you call that thing a '*window*' or a '*ventana*' or a '*mado*' or even 'a hole in the wall,' is irrelevant. Those are just different labels attached to the same thing." This view seems sensible enough, even far more sophisticated than the semantic notion that there is only one correct name for each thing in the universe. But the commonsense view can be challenged.

The view can be challenged even by a curious child who asks, "Where does my lap go when I stand up?" Or, "Where does my fist go when I open my hand?" Try, for a moment, to answer these questions and you may learn something about your own semantic sophistication.

I have asked such questions to college students in the United States and in Japan and have found a marked difference in the answers given. A large percentage of American students reply with answers that seem to reflect an uneasiness with the question and a patronizing attitude toward children. So we get answers like, "Your lap slides down your legs into your socks," or "Your fist flies around waiting until you close your hand again." The answers given by bilingual students in Japan whose first language is Japanese are quite different. "'Lap' is a word used to describe this part of your body when it is in this position; so if you change the position, of course, you don't need to use that word." Comparable answers are given to the question about the fist.

Why the difference? Culturally, the Japanese can be at least as patronizing toward children as can their American counterparts, and in many respects the Japanese students are no more sensitive or sophisticated about semantics than the Americans. The reason for the difference seems to be quite simple: in the Japanese language there is no word equivalent to "lap," and no word equivalent to "fist." As the students learned English they were quite aware of the arbitrariness of naming, in these cases the naming of temporary positions of parts of the body. (Native English speakers who are learning Japanese face comparable problems, of course—there is but a single word for both "arm" and "hand," and another word for both "leg" and "foot," etc.) When one studies general semantics one, in a sense, seeks to discover the arbitrariness of his own native language and the associations of his own language habits, much as one inevitably discovers these in learning another language. That kind of awareness can help us avoid at least some kinds of subtle semantic traps, particularly of the kind in which a word is mistaken for a thing.

The cultural anthropologist, Dorothy Lee, has articulated the case against the neat duality of "words" and "things" in drawing upon her knowledge of North American Indian languages. [7] Follow her reasoning as she pursues the question with reference to a hand holding a pencil:

> According the the classical view, the word is not the *thing*. This object that I hold in my hand is independent of the label I give it. It *is* not a pencil; I only assign to it the name pencil. What *it is*, is assumed to be independent of what *I call it*. Pencil is only a sound-complex, a word for the reality, the *thing*. But . . . when I call this "pencil," I also classify it, as a substantive, a noun; I separate it as other than the fingers it elongates. Is it a *thing* before I call it a pencil?

Note that Lee is *not* asking if that object (pencil) exists or if it can be perceived or any other such question. She asks only, "Is it a *thing* before I call it a pencil?" She continues.

> If it is not, then I am not "applying" a name to an already existing thing. This physical reality, this formless mass or energy, or set of relations, is delimited, is given form and substance, becomes the *thing* pencil, only through my calling it a pencil. A Maidu Indian, for example, would probably have given no recognition to, or would not have delimited this reality into, the pencil as object; instead, he would have perceived the specific act of the hand—in this case the act of pointing with a pencil—and would have expressed this by means of a suffix which, attached to the verb, "to point," means: to-point-with-a-long-thin-instrument (such as a pencil or a straight pipe, or a cigarette, or a stick). There is no reference to substance or to an object in this suffix. What is a pencil to me is a qualification or an attribute of an act for him, and belongs to a class with cigarettes and other objects of this shape only in so far as they elongate the hand making such an act possible. If this can be called a *thing*, then the symbolic process has at any rate helped create different *things* out of the physical reality.
>
> I would say, therefore, that the classical *this* is not the *thing*, but the reality itself. At the point where it is a *thing*, it has already been made into a thing. The word and the thing are not discrete elements to be

[7] Dorothy Lee, "Symbolization and Value," in *Freedom and Culture* (Englewood Cliff, N.J.: Prentice-Hall, 1959), p. 80.

24   *Semantics and Communication*

related by the speaker; they are interdependent, incapable of existence apart from and without the act of the individual.

This more sophisticated position of interdependence between word and thing seems preferable to the assumption, stated at the beginning of the chapter, of words and things being completely separate. When we say "the word is not the thing," we have already begged the question—for what was the *thing* in the first place? We would have had to *assume the existence of a discrete "thing."* Now our revised assumption is that the idea of the "thing" can come about only through symbolization. This revised position should not be confused with philosophies that deny the existence of reality entirely; nor should we think that if we have no word for "wall" we won't bump into something if we walk into what the word "wall" would symbolize. We would still be stopped by something in reality, but how we would *describe* that collision would be different. In short, "reality" is a stimulus that we shape into many "things" through symbolization (language). As soon as we talk about the "things" of the world we have already given shape to that stimulus.

In the light of the developments of the philosophy of science in this century, such a view is not surprising. When the scientist began to realize that it was *he* who *"made* sense" of the world and that what he had regarded as "discoveries" might have been better called "inventions" or "conveniences," a completely new attitude and approach resulted.

> For centuries it was thought that the theorems of Euclid were conceptual photographs, so to speak, of the external world, that they had a validity quite independent of the human mind; that there was something necessary and inevitable about them. The invention of non-Euclidean geometries by Lobatchewsky, Riemann and others has dispelled this view entirely. It is now clear that concepts such as space, straight line, plane, etc., are no more necessary and inevitable as a consequence of the structure of the external world than are the concepts green and yellow—or the relationship term with which you designate your mother's brother, for that matter.
>
> To quote Einstein . . . "We come now to the question: what is *a priori* certain or necessary in geometry (doctrine of space) or its founda-

tions? Formerly we thought everything; nowadays we think—nothing. Already the distance-concept is logically arbitrary; there need be no things that correspond to it, even approximately."[8]

This attitude cannot be overemphasized, for it is popularly thought that somehow the scientist (or, worse, Science) sees the world "as it really is." Superstitious or misinformed ideas about the scientist in his laboratory portray him as one without bias, without the perceptual distortions characteristic of the rest of us poor souls. But this is not so. The scientist no more sees what is "really there" than does a mystic or poet or taxi driver. What the scientist does that most others do not is *to be aware of what he is doing*—at least to the best of his ability. Thus aware, he can tell others *how* he came to see what he saw and what they must do to see the world the same way. It is the rigor of the *method* of observation that distinguishes the tradition of science from other traditions that have made special claims for seeing the real world. The scientist is not blessed or superhuman; he is only careful.

Language, from Free Speech to Newspeak

One of the most fascinating speculative treatments on semantics appears in George Orwell's novel, *1984*, particularly in the appendix to the book which describes "the principles of newspeak." In that grim police state where Big Brother is everywhere, the primary instrument of control is not the police but rather *language*. Based on the assumption that what one cannot speak he cannot think, one of the characteristics of newspeak is to decrease the size of the dictionary year after year. A word like "free" might for a time be used to say "the field is free of weeds" or "the dog is free of fleas," but the language makes it impossible to express a human desire to be free. There are other more detailed explanations of how the language of newspeak works, and the reader is urged to examine them himself. They are partly Orwell's own invention and partly his satire on

[8] Leslie A. White, "The Locus of Mathematical Reality: An Anthropological Footnote," in James R. Newman (ed.), *The World of Mathematics* (New York: Simon and Schuster, 1956), Vol. IV, p. 2354.

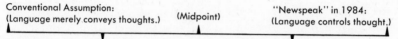

Conventional Assumption: "Newspeak" in 1984:
(Language merely conveys thoughts.)   (Midpoint)   (Language controls thought.)

Chomsky and the transformational linguists   Sapir, Whorf, Dorothy Lee, etc.

trends he felt were already underway in England thirty years ago. They also represent a point of view about the role of language in influencing thought and action that is taken seriously by many scholars, though rarely to the degree that Orwell suggested. We can think of the newspeak of 1984 as representing one extreme on a continuum of language and thought relationships, one which sees language as *the* predominant influence in perception, thought, and behavior.

The other extreme on this continuum needs no book or organized theory to represent it, for that view is the conventional, "naive" assumption that language is a neutral medium through which "thought" is expressed and "reality" identified. It was the view that went almost unchallenged by philosophers and language scholars until about the turn of the century.

If we mark a place midway along this continuum we will have a point of reference from which to place two other views which we have mentioned previously in this book. Somewhere between that midpoint and the traditional view of language and thought relationships we might place the dominant school of American linguists, represented by Noam Chomsky. Between that midpoint and the extreme view in the fictional 1984 we can mark the position stated by Dorothy Lee and other anthropological linguists whom we will consider shortly. Let us briefly look at these positions.

There is impresssive evidence that each individual is biologically equipped to generate utterances in accordance with the language spoken by those around him, but not limited to mere repetition of what he has heard. Children can construct statements that are novel even while conforming to the general rules of their "mother tongue." The time and stages of first language learning appear to be the same for children all over the world, irrespective of their particular language. Both of these observations suggest to some that the most obvious differences in language are not as significant as some people might think; there is, if you will, a universality of man that is revealed even in language. Most important in the view of this school of linguists, however, is the theory that anything said in any one language can, if it is examined at a "deeper level" (that is, not at the "surface" level of expression), be transformed into comparable expressions in any other language. I suspect that linguists who accept this view of language would still go along with much of the concerns of the general semanticists while denying that the root of the trouble lies in language. They would not, however, agree with the reasoning of Dorothy Lee.

Lee, of course, places far more stress on the influence of language (or symbolization)—though not to the extent that Orwell conjectured in his novel. Lee is one anthropologist who is a part of a much larger, and better known, group of scholars with whom the general semantics school is most often identified. This school of thought is identified with various names—"linguistic relativism," and sometimes "linguistic determinism," but most frequently by the names of individuals who have advanced such views. These include von Humboldt and particularly the American linguist Edward Sapir and his student Benjamin Lee Whorf. In its simplest form the "Sapir–Whorf hypothesis" states that what we perceive and how we think is restricted by the particular language we speak. Thus a speaker of English and a native speaker of Hopi do not live in the same perceptual world, even if they happen to live in neighboring villages. We have no choice but to follow the dictates of our language, and languages differ considerably in how they symbolize "reality."

Unfortunately, it is no more possible to prove that "language shapes our perception of reality" than to prove the opposite, more conventional, view. Some languages, including English, require that we speak of events in the past or the present or the future; in English we cannot speak of an event in those three tenses all at once. In some other languages, Whorf demonstrates, there is no such three-part division of time. But because in such examples we are comparing languages and translations of languages—not "perception" and certainly not "pure thought"—we are still not proving the hypothesis. And for some scholars that is sufficient reason to ignore the hypothesis. For others, this writer included, a judgment by Mark Twain applies to this subtle but important issue: "interesting, if true . . . and interesting, anyway."

THREE
WORDS, WORDS, WORDS. . .

Learning the Language

The first breath of life is often noisy. This noise continues, except during rest, until the last breath, but the quality and purpose of human sounds undergo great changes, especially in the first two years. During these first twenty-four months the rudiments of a language are obtained and the flesh is made human. At three months the child begins its career of babbling, which usually reaches a peak in another four months. By the time the baby blows out its first birthday candle it is prepared to imitate adult noises. Within another half year it can utter several single-word sentences, and by the age of two its sentences include pronouns, articles, conjunctions, and prepositions. By the age of five the child knows the sound and structure of its language better than most foreign students with years of training, even if the child's vocabulary is less extensive.

How the child learns all of this is either clearly known or little known, depending on how specific an explanation one seeks. Both babies and chimpanzees are vocally equipped to do the same thing, both are notorious mimics, but in the presence of adult speakers only the child learns a language. As discussed in the first chapter, the crucial difference between baby chimpanzee and baby *Homo sapiens* seems to reside in the larger cortex of the human infant. Nevertheless, it is imitation that elicits language. The few isolated (and unreliable) cases of infants that have survived away from human world indicates that a child cannot teach itself to learn language or in any way "become human."

The child imitates what it sees and hears, without being aware of what all of this is about, and is rewarded when the imitation is a good one and is discouraged when the imitation is off the mark. If the child could utter an adult platitude in those early months it might say, "I don't know much about language, but I know what I like," for it is the affectionate reenforcement it receives and not any conscious awareness of what it is doing that eventually produces language. The child learns by receiving a smile or a kiss or a spoonful of applesauce for saying "doggie" when one thing passes before it and saying "Daddy" when something else is there. At the outset the child knows nothing of strings of words or sentences; it merely imitates the sounds as best it can. To the young child, the sound of "kitty" and "look at kitty" differ only in difficulty of expression, not semantically. For this reason, children who for awhile may seem to understand certain words and phrases later prove to know only how to repeat them. A young child may seem to be able to correctly identify "Daddy" because the only adults he regularly sees are "Daddy" and "Mommy." It comes as a surprise when the child begins to call the milkman, the mailman, and the meter reader "Daddy," too. It is not that the child cannot distinguish his progenitor from other male visitors, but rather that his verbal associations are too general. A noted writer tells of the time when he and his family lived near a park that featured an equestrian statue of General Grant. The statue was a favorite of his daughter, who was told that it was called "Grant." Eventually it was necessary for the family to move elsewhere, and before leaving, the little girl asked her father if she could go to the park to say good-bye to Grant. This she did, saying "Good-bye, Grant, good-bye, Grant." Later she asked her father, "Daddy, who was that soldier riding Grant?"

The process of learning to make socially meaningful noises and to interpret those of other speakers continues throughout life. The most basic vocabulary and structure is learned through repetition and reenforcement in the earliest years, so that it is unlikely that you can recall when you first learned to use most of the words you use every day. A vocabulary that is taught formally, with attention to definitions (meanings-in-other-words) comes later. It is quite possible, for example, that you can remember when you first learned such words as *photosynthesis* or *protagonist* or *paleolithic*. Your associations with such words may include former school teachers, spelling contests, or browsings through an encyclopedia. Such words, unlike those of your basic vocabulary, are perhaps more easily defined than used. From the point of view of semantics, usage and meaning are ultimately difficult to distinguish, but in the process of growing up and learning a language the distinction is apparent.

It should be pointed out that the process of learning a language *for a child* is the same everywhere, for every language. No one's first language is harder or easier to learn than any other. The age and sequence of language learning is the same everywhere. Even if children have had some illness that retarded their language learning, once their problem is corrected they proceed along the same pattern, for this process, it now seems clear, is biologically based. (At puberty, however, the brain, as well as the more visible parts of the body, undergoes a significant change; one effect of that change is to make future language learning, such as studying a foreign language, both different and far more difficult.)

In the past decade or so, the work of Eric Lenneberg and Noam Chomsky have contributed greatly to our understanding of how a person comes to learn and use his language. The thrust of both scholars has been to emphasize the universality of language, Lenneberg, in terms of physiology and biology and Chomsky, the noted linguist, in terms of underlying structures of language. In the past it had been thought that we learned our language solely through imitation, what Roger Brown has called "the original word game," played between adults and children. [1] Obviously imitation is crucial—we learn the language spoken by our parents or those around us and not any other language. However, it has become clear that what we say, even as children, is not limited to mere

[1] Roger Brown, *Words and Things* (Glencoe, Ill.: Free Press, 1958), pp. 194–228.

imitation; we make all kinds of sentences that we have never learned said. So it seems that a more accurate view of language learning is that we learn *principles* from which we *generate* new, often unique, utterances.

Those linguists who have followed Chomsky's thinking believe that the underlying principles of grammar are comparable in all languages. That is, although the surface expressions of a language may seem quite different, we have only to go beneath the surface to an underlying structure to find ways of transforming expressions of one language into expressions of another or to find the rules for generating unique utterances which are within our own language. Hence the name for this school, the transformational generative grammarians.

When my daughter was very little she once asked her mother, "Are you happy at me?" Apparently she had learned some rule based on "Are you angry at me?" and evolved a new expression. Chomsky, like most linguists, is primarily concerned with the *syntactic* aspect of language which we mentioned in Chapter One. But the implications of his work might be significant for the pragmatic aspects which are the major concern of our study of semantics. If one is learning primarily learning principles, and if these underlying principles seem to be either similar or at least interchangeable in all languages all over the world, why should we assume that our language or language habits influence the way we think and act? This is a major issue and marks a departure from some of the basic assumptions of Korzybski many years ago.

That "original word game," establishes not only the basis for socialization, but also for all of thinking and even much of perceiving. In some sense, then, children are partially correct when they believe as they do that people think with their mouths and ears. [2] By locating thinking in these areas, the child at least calls attention to the influence of language on thought. To this extent the description may be preferable to the common belief of many adults in the existence of some organ called "the mind."

Unaware of the influence of language and the rather arbitrary

---

[2] Jean Piaget, *The Child's Conception of the World* (Paterson, N.J.: Littlefield, Adams & Co., 1929, 1963), p. 38.

way in which they have learned theirs, mature individuals may carry with them all their lives the patterns established in infancy. More committed to language habits than they are aware of and continuing to associate words and things, they may remain "infantile" in their thinking and behavior. It was such a position that Korzybski took when he developed his theory of a general semantics.[3] His assumptions of the child's language habits that remain influential in the adult's life are consistent with what others have discovered, and cannot be dismissed. And although our goal in this book is not therapy, we will have occasion to return to these assumptions throughout the remainder of this book.

The First Dimension of Language

The Convention of Naming. The child learns that everything has a name and that these names must be very important to his parents because every time the child makes one kind of noise in association with a thing his parents like it, and when he makes another kind of noise they do not seem much impressed. This training continues for years. Children love it because they are learning to do something very adult, and adults love it because they appear to be experts at it. The early rewards for correctly naming a thing are later replaced by other symbolic rewards—by gold stars in grade school, later by high marks, and eventually by certificates and diplomas of various kinds. Throughout life, being able to *name*—which is to say being able to make verbal distinctions that somebody regards as correct and important—is greatly admired. Naming may be *the* universal pastime. Naming is also the first dimension of language.

Naming is a convention. We should note right away that there is no necessary relationship between the sound of a word (or shape, if the word is printed) and what the word stands for.

[3] The extent to which the general semantics of Korzybski was correct and useful or greatly exaggerated is yet to be determined. His ambition of a universal therapy through semantic awareness has not been realized, and his methods have been soundly criticized. One of the most intelligent criticisms of Korzybski, free of the polemics that have characterized so many writers pro and con general semantics, appears in John Carroll's *The Study of Language* (Cambridge, Mass.: Harvard Univ. Press, 1963), pp. 164–168.

There have been studies in phonetic symbolism which show that even in very different languages, given a pair of nonsense words and imaginary references to which to apply these words, people tend to agree on how to match the sound with the "thing." All over the world, "*gik*" sounds like something lighter or smaller than a "*guk*," for example. And there is also the class of words called onomatopoeia, where the sound of the word is an attempt to imitate a natural sound. Attractive as this might seem, there are problems. For one thing our vocabulary tends to be much more visual than oral: we simply don't or can't conceptualize very much on the basis of sound. (What is the sound of a desk or a chair or a book?) Also, if we compare languages we find that even the words that attempt to imitate sounds, such as dogs barking or bells ringing, are different in different languages. The words used to describe the sound of a dog barking in Greek is very close to the word used in English to describe a turkey gobbling.

If we desired, and everybody agreed to the change, we could call this book a "spaghetti" and could call spaghetti "book." If the change were consistent, no confusion would result. Indeed, over many years the referents for certain sounds (words) do change, but because speakers learn the changes at the same time there is no confusion. That the word *girl* once meant a young person of either sex or that the word *coast* was formerly applied to any border (Switzerland used to have a "coast") says something about the convention of naming and not about the history of girls, boys, and borders.

We make rapid symbolic changes all of the time. For example, in playing card games the Queen of Spades "means" thirteen points in the game of hearts and means ten points in blackjack. We don't argue about what the sound of *queen* really should mean; we simply agree to a meaning for the particular game and enjoy ourselves. It is this very flexibility that permits us to play so many games with only fifty-two cards. The same is true of the language game. So long as we are all playing by the same rules, using words in more or less the same ways, we can communicate reasonably well.

What we learn to call the things of this world is largely a result of our social and educational background. Whether you learn to "eat dinner" or "take dinner" says something about the social values your family has placed on these words. Whether you call a particular paper container a *bag* or a *sack* may depend on the part of the United States in which you have been reared (or *raised*).

Children who are instructed in what to call things and are corrected when they do not name objects in the same way that their parents do often come to believe that there are correct names and incorrect names, and there is always just one to a customer. Perhaps the majority of children who ask "Why is the sun called the sun?" are told, "because that's what it is." (If they ask again, they may receive the same answer in a slightly louder voice.) Under such instruction the child's attitude can be understood. Without an awareness of the nature of his language the adult remains, in this sense, a child all of his life. One of the most common and most childish of adult arguments is the disagreement over what something "should be called," or what something "*really* is."

In one sense, the parent is correct when he tells his child who asks why something is called what it is called, "because that's what it is called." (The adult should not say "because it *has* to be called that" or "because that is what it *is*," of course.) When one learns a language, whether it is his first or his second or tenth, it is not for him to ask *why* something is called what it is called. Etymology is a fascinating study, but it does not help one to speak a language or understand other speakers. Imitate others and play the word game. That is what we have all done, and that is basically what enables you to understand anything verbal, like this book.

Everything Has a Name.   The ability to give a name to everything often passes for education. It is a common belief that to be able to name something is to know it; to define something is to "truly understand it." Neither assumption is correct, of course. There are dull and pedantic persons who have large vocabularies, and there are imaginative, perceptive individuals whose lexicon is limited. Despite such evidence, the belief that the more you can name the more you know persists. The explanation of language training and reward previously cited partially explain this.

The naming itself is not a problem, for naming is the basis of language. Rather, it is the erroneous attitudes about naming and the exaggerated influence of names that are sometimes problematic.

Among the common mistaken attitudes about names is that each "thing" has only one correct name. As indicated in the previous section, names are only matters of convention and convenience, and they change with the times. The one-thing–one-name assumption is not borne out.

Perhaps the most pervasive criticism of the obsession for naming that characterizes much of Western language and thought (based in culture, not language) is the need to know names in order to recognize experiences, and the corresponding attitude that experiences that are not named are irrelevant. How many persons can enjoy a find piece of music without wishing to identify the composer and title? How many can enjoy the first balmy spring day without desiring to know the exact temperature? Or enjoy a piece of nonrepresentational art without knowing what it is called, even if the name be only "Perspectives" or "Number 17"?

It is this exaggerated importance of naming every event, every experience, every thing perceived as distinct that is often disturbing. We seem most obsessed where the names and information are often the least important, as in our statistical treatment of most sporting events. Few persons seem to realize that we could name as many things as we wanted to. Like the specialist or hobbyist who, to the uninitiated, seems to talk in code, we could produce elaborate lists of names for "things" that have never been named. Such lists would be useless, of course, for the value of naming lies in its efficient notation of what is important and the way relationships can be indicated.

Once names are learned, at least two effects may result. One is the feedback effect on perception. *We begin to notice those things for which we have names*. Before taking a course in astronomy, you may have looked into the sky on a clear evening and seen only stars. After a few weeks of study you do not see "stars"—instead you see (or say you see) supernovae, white dwarfs, galaxies. Your responses to what you see may include a new and thrilling sense of distance and perspective, including a sense of your own insignificance in so vast a universe. Of course this results from knowing not just the names of the points of light in the sky but also how they are related and what you have learned about them. But such meanings must follow the symbolic distinctions among what had previously seemed to be all "just stars." Thus, for better or for worse, when names are learned we see what we had not seen, for we know what to look for.

A second result of naming, which may at first appear to contradict the previous effect, is *the failure to see things once we have names*. To take the previous example through another step, suppose that we had never learned that what was in the sky were called "stars" because we had never bothered to look up at night. Then one clear summer's evening we cast our eyes upward and behold!—what do we see? It is possible that we will see only "stars," but it is also possible that we notice that the points of light up there do *not* all look alike. Lacking a single name for that range of brightness and color, we might notice differences and thus never assume that they were all alike in the first place.

This seems paradoxical. In one case, learning names helps us to "see" what we had not noticed. In another case, learning names seems to blind us to what we would have seen if we hadn't learned the name. How can this be resolved?

Both possibilities exist in our behavior all of the time. As we learn to name "things" we abstract certain characteristics in order to apply a single name to a variety of experiences, be they stars or breakfast foods. It would be impossible to have a language if every experience (defined in time and space) had to have a new name, and so we classify groups. In doing this we blind ourselves to the individual differences within the group. Later, as our education (and vocabulary) increase we begin to identify some of those differences. In many instances we notice so many differences within what we had considered as one group previously that we no longer find the original single term very useful. This is exactly what happens when we pursue special interests. At the age of four all things that creep or crawl may have been identified for us as *bugs*. By the time we finish a biology unit in grade school the term *bugs* may not seem very convenient, and if we were to do graduate work in entomology the term *bugs* would be completely useless as a general term for insects.

It is impossible to know what distinctions a child makes before it learns language. William James' description of the infant's world as "One blooming, buzzing confusion" is as good a guess as any. This is usually taken to mean that the child has not learned to conceive of himself as a self apart from what surrounds him or to develop perfected perceptual skills for identification. It might also be interpreted as indicating the child is supersensitive to so many distinctions in the world about him that it cannot function, and that the first stages of language serve to dull this sensitivity and permit only socially meaningful distinctions to be made. Here we are in the realm of speculation, which is unnecessary to pursue further for our purposes.

This section may be summarized by noting that we learn to make verbal distinctions for the things around us. To the extent that our distinctions are gross, with many differences omitted, the process of naming may dull our sensitivities. To the extent that names remind us to look for distinctions we had not noted before learning the names, naming increases our sensitivity. When naming becomes so obsessive that we are discomforted when we cannot name an experience or when we think that a name is the most important characteristic of an experience, we are indeed confused. And so we are, most of us some of the time, confused.

The Elemental Problem. Although elementalism in semantics may be regarded as an aspect of the previous section, it deserves special attention. By elementalism is meant the effect of arbitrarily imposing a static language on a process-reality that we experience. Elementalism calls attention to the linguistic division of the indivisible experiences of our lives.

As we begin to use words we begin to abstract "characteristics" of a "single experience." If we take for an example one specific experience that might correspond to what we would label *a hot day*, our *experience* is not one of *hot* and another of *day. Our experience is one*—we could not have had *that* day without the *hot*, too. However, if language is to be efficient we must use relatively few words for an unlimited number of experiences, and so we distinguish our abstractions for use in many experiences. This is the convenience and necessity of language. What must be recognized is that only the *words* are repeated in other combinations, not the experiences. If this observation seems strange or confusing it may be that you have become so accustomed to your language that you assume that words must have a one-to-one correspondence to experience. You assume that if there is a word *hot* there must be *a discrete "thing"* that is "hot," and so on.

Because our language requires us to organize our words in certain patterns as we would thread beads on a string or stack building blocks one on top of the other, we cannot avoid some form of elementalism. We can, however, be aware of what we are doing and know that this is a necessary evil of language and not a mirror of reality in our experience.

The elementalistic problems of language that can more easily be attended to are those arbitrary divisions that may have once made sense but which, in the light of recent descriptions in science, no longer appear to. Einstein's contribution to semantics was an attack on the division between time and space. In some time in the future we may no longer speak of the two as separate elements in our language. The traditional distinctions between mind and body, between ends and means, between material and spiritual, and so on, appear to be much weaker in this century than they have been traditionally. When the experiences they would describe are investigated carefully, the student finds that such distinctions are either meaningless or deceptive.

An important change occurred in the history of Western thought when philosophers and scientists stopped describing the world in terms of separate elements and began to describe relationships in process. The physicist stopped looking for an element called "heat" and began to study therm*odynamics*.

The approaches of "transactional psychology," "general systems theory," and other related fields which have attracted attention in recent years also reflect a shift from individual persons and things to relationships. Thus a therapist today may realize that a "problem child" in a family may only be a person identified as such by others; "the problem," however, may lie in the relationships between that person and the others in the family or, indeed, in a larger segment of society. Viewed in this way, the entire family may require counseling, not just the identified child. To effectively treat "alcoholism" or "hypertension" might require a kind of "treatment" for a whole network of social systems and behavior, for these problems are not individual problems that reside within people but manifestations of relationships at a level that is vast and complex. An increasing number of doctors today are viewing problems of "heatlth" in this way. [4]

"Health" as it is most frequently viewed in the United States today, and even as defined by the World Health Organization, appears as an ideal state that resides within an individual. [5] But, as critics have pointed out, not only is such an idealized state almost impossible to achieve or maintain, "it" is contingent upon relationships which are constantly changing. We may say that a person "has his health" in Chicago but that he "loses it" when he goes to the altitude of Denver or the heat of Arizona. We *can* talk about "health" that way, as if it were an "it" to be possessed or lost, but a more sensible description would be in terms of an individual's neurophysiological system in relationship to his surroundings. "Health" is a limited description of an ever-changing process, not a *thing*.

In our social relations, especially, the change from an elementalistic to a process attitude has been most important. The field of *group dynamics*, which reflects the attitude in its title, regards terms such as *leader*, *deviant member*, *true partner*, and *cohesiveness*, not as separate moving parts in a machine, but as inseparable relationships of a group. In describing any conversation you cannot talk about one without talking about the others. If one member of a group is removed or another added, you do not just change the number of persons in the group, you change the nature and process of the whole group. In the home, if Grandma comes to live with the family, you do not just "add Grandma," you establish a new pattern of relationships. You no longer have the previous experience plus Grandma, you have something entirely new. Similarly, if a member of the family dies, you cannot just "subtract one"; obviously, there is an entirely new pattern of behavior to which you must adapt.

When one distorts his understanding of the process experience by regarding what words stand for as static elements that can be

---

[4] See, for example, Andrew Melleson, *The Medical Run-around* (N.Y.: Hart, 1974).

[5] The W.H.O. definition of "health" is "a state of complete physical, mental, and social well-being, and not merely the absence of disease of infirmity."

added or subtracted, he may also think of these elements as palpable things that have shape and substance. The child believes that one may touch thought. [6] The word *thought* fits into the same sentence patterns as nouns for material objects, and we retain, at least metaphorically, the idea of *thought* as a *thing* even as adults. We speak of "having a few thoughts," or, in a peculiar animalistic cliché, of something being "food for thought."

One interesting and significant treatment of process as elements is especially American and recent. This is our attitude toward time. Perhaps the vast majority of Americans believe that *time* consists of something they can save, waste, spend, keep, and so on. "If you save an hour today you will have it tomorrow," we may say. But one hour today is not the same hour tomorrow. Time at the age of twenty-one is not time after sixty-five.

In summary, we should note that the elementalistic bias is necessary in language, for words mark off arbitrary distinctions that do not exist in the reality they represent. However, when we fail to recognize this as a necessary evil of language and instead believe that reality is composed of elements that correspond to our vocabulary, we are abused by our language. What can be altered without altering the nature and structure of our language are the gross dichotomies ("mind and body," and so on) that are neither consistent with contemporary knowledge nor particularly useful. We can also avoid describing our experiences in terms of simple mathematics, adding and subtracting "attributes" to or from a "basic experience." All are parts of the whole, and to change any one changes all of the rest.

Language, Values, and Culture

It is impossible to fully distinguish language from the culture in which it appears. Nor can one speak of culture without speaking of its underlying values. And without some understanding of cultural values one cannot appreciate the meanings of words as they are used

[6] Jean Piaget, *The Child's Conception of the World* (Paterson, N.J.: Littlefield, Adams & Co., 1929, 1963), pp. 38–49.

in that culture. In the United States, for example, usually "yes" means yes, "no" means no: we value being blunt, practical, objective. In Japan, on the other hand, interpersonal relations are often more important than "objectivity," and indirection, vagueness, or ambiguity are far more valued than bluntness of speech. So in Japan you rarely hear the equivalent of "no," at least not if saying "no" might disappoint somebody. One student has catalogued at least eighteen ways of avoiding saying "no" directly, even though in most of these cases the listener fully understands that something like "no" is meant. And if it should come to a "yes-or-no" situation some Japanese will switch into English to state such a crude choice.

Of course, no Japanese-English dictionary will explain this sort of thing; it is not a matter of simple semantics. Nor is there anything in the language, Japanese or English or any other, which would account for this. We must look at the more general semantics of the culture, including the values which underlie and govern the use of expressions.

It has long been noted that what is valued in a culture or within a smaller group within a culture will be reflected in vocabulary. As a general rule the more words a language has for certain concepts, the more important are those concepts. Arabic used to have several thousand words to refer to the camel, but as the importance of the camel has waned, the word stock has also decreased. Where there are technological developments, inventions, and innovations, our vocabulary is likely to reflect such developments. Consider the number of words we use for kinds of medicine or music or shoes or automobiles. Our vocabulary both reflects and directs our attention to making finer distinctions than other people make who have no such interest or knowledge. Slang and in-group speech is also an index of what is important. This kind of speech, characteristic of any subgroup, serves the members in two ways: it serves to symbolically distinguish the "in people" from the "out people," the people who talk like us from the people who talk like outsiders; and in that talking it serves to reinforce the interests and perceptions of reality that characterize the group. The same can be said for a culture as a whole. The often-discussed generation gap is revealed at least as clearly in the speaking habits of those from different generations as by other characteristics of their life styles. Indeed, it might be possible to distinguish one generation from another solely on the basis of speaking—what is talked about, what expressions are used or not used, and so on. In English we can say: "atheistic Communism," "act like a lady," "rip off," "a darling dress" and "capitalist exploitation." And yet except for parody or sarcasm it is unlikely that any one speaker will use all of these expressions. Each reflects a view of reality, a symbolic demarcation of what is valued or not, and probably some identification with other speakers as well. In the United States in recent years, there appears to have developed more and more subgroups, special interest groups, and maybe even more of a tolerance for differences in life styles. The communications media have aided this fragmentation, if that is what it is, so that records or newspapers or even grand rituals (such as Woodstock) serve to convey and maintain the symbols of unity among these groups. Alvin Toffler in his remarkable book, *Future Shock*, has projected this pattern far into the future. [7] One effect of this development is to alter the concept of "culture" from a physical setting (such as equivalent to a nation or an ethnic group within a nation) to a more widespread network. Perhaps the Beatles or Bob Dylan back in the 1960s best exemplified this tendency as their music influenced the language and symbol systems of young people all over the wo:ld. There was a kind of "Beatles culture" that cut across borders, oceans, and even languages. There were other identifications, "youth culture," "counterculture," "hip culture," and so on, too, which—in dress, hair style, as well as in words—symbolically created new unions and divided older ones. The phenomenon continues and as a result we may have to revise our notions of both culture and of language.

However we define "culture," it should be clear that the distinctions of any one culture are not more "correct" than those of another. Each is useful for the culture in which it appears. Within a single culture the principle is the same. In certain fields the U.S. chemist does not make the same distinctions that a U.S. plumber would make. But the distinctions important to the English-speaking chemist may be very much the same as the distinctions important to a German-speaking chemist, for within the "culture" of chemistry,

[7] Alvin Toffler, *Future Shock* (New York: Random House, 1971).

these distinctions have meaning. It is not "correctness" but "utility" that is the criterion.

If one raised the academic question about naming, "What is the *best* name for X?" the answer could not be given until another question was answered: "What do you have in mind?" Entertainer Steve Allen was once asked by a reporter whether he considered himself to be essentially a comedian, a musician, a writer, or what? He replied that when he told jokes he was a comedian, when he played the piano he was a musician, when he wrote he was an author, and when he cut the grass he was a lawn mower. Allen's deft reply is a lesson in semantics. What something "should be called" depends, in part, on the use one wishes to make of it or a particular point of view one has toward it. An item is a piece of *mail* in the mailbox, *advertising* when we read it, and *trash* when we throw it away.

Any one "thing" becomes many "things" depending on what you call it and, hence, how you look at it. Take the object you are looking at now, for example. You may classify it as "a book," and because of other objects that also fit into that category you know some of the things you can do with it. Because you regard it as *a book* you assume, without putting it to a test, that you can read it or put it on a shelf. Suppose, however, you needed to write a telephone number in a hurry and could not find a blank piece of paper. You might reclassify the book as a *source of paper* and use it for that purpose. Such a use might not have occurred to you at the time you purchased the book ("books are for reading and shelving"), but might occur later. If loose papers were blowing on the desk you might classify the book as an *object heavier than a sheet of paper* and use it as a paperweight. This nonverbal object usually classified as *book* could be reclassified and used as a door prop, a decoration, a weapon, an apparatus for achieving better posture, or part of that most ambiguous classification *a well-read man*. How we classify any object or event suggests a use, a purpose. If a person thinks only in terms of one possible classification for any object, his behavior may be limited by his use of language.

There is good evidence that the most imaginative persons are those who are not bound by a single classification for an object or situation. That children are often more "creative" than adults may be because, lacking a comprehensive vocabulary, they are freer to treat objects as objects, not as classifications. A child may amuse himself for hours with some pots and pans because he has not bound his thinking to "cooking utensils." Adults might be bored by that entertainment but might also feel silly—for everybody knows that "pots are for cooking" and not for playing.

In summary, the first dimension of language, naming, contains a utilitarian bias. When we assume that one name (and its implied purpose) is the only, best, most appropriate, name we take our learning too seriously. Or perhaps not seriously enough. Any one "thing" may be many symbolic "things," depending on our attitudes. Problems result when we fail to recognize this and associate word and thing so consistently that we think that what we usually call something is what it *really* is.[8]

The Second Dimension of Language

The child begins learning his language by discovering that everything has a name. This is what we have called the first dimension of language, the consistent association of one name with some thing. But the child may soon discover that "one thing" can have more than one name and that one word can stand for more than one thing. Suppose the child learns that the furry, noisy thing that licks his face is called *dog*. It is also called *Spot*. He has also heard his parents call the dog a *pet*. And he once heard his father shout, "Get that animal out of my bedroom!" And the *animal* turned out to be *Spot*. If he were an attentive child he might hear that thing called all of these names (including *that thing*) during any one day. At the point where he learns that all of these names can refer to the same thing but that some of the words include many other things as well,

---

[8] One of the greatest problems in international relations is the imposition of classifications that are meaningful in one culture onto another culture where they may not be meaningful. The ethnocentric attitude that demands that "they" see things "our way" (often disguised as the "modern," "correct," "ideal," or "practical" way) is a semantic problem of the gravest importance today. Mastering the motor skills of another language is a simple task compared to the "mastery" of the semantic reactions appropriate to another culture.

he is learning about the second dimension of language; in the terminology of semantics, he is learning that words are on different levels of abstraction.

Levels of Abstraction.   The concept of different *levels* of abstraction is nothing new. In rather sophisticated ways, logicians and epistemologists have been aware for centuries that some words are more specific than others. Any discussion of categories, subcategories and categories of categories (even preceding Aristotle) makes this clear. What is new and what the semanticists have emphasized is that higher levels of abstraction are farther from sense data, and therefore a person who responds in the same way to a low-level abstraction (this-dog-Spot) as to a higher level abstraction (animal) is acting in a peculiar way. Korzybski went further. He labeled such reactions "unsane," for he reasoned that to respond to words that stand for many other *words* in the same way you react to words that stand for *things* indicates a confusion between word and thing. Such behavior is out of the realm of sense-data reality and in a world of words.[9]

To clarify the notion of levels of abstraction, look at the object that contains the page you are presently reading. Without uttering a word about it or giving it a name, observe it. Handle it. This is the sense-data that you can label *Semantics and Communication*. You may also label it a *textbook*, in which case it receives the same name as any of several other sense-data objects in your room. Or you can call it a *book*, which is a little more general than *textbook*, for the word *book* includes those things that you enjoy reading. Or you can call it *printed matter*, a classification that also includes newspapers

---

[9] This attitude is based on an assumption that dates at least to the Thirteenth-Century conflict between the *nominalists* and the *realists*. The nominalists (including not only the present-day semanticists, but also those in the tradition of the scientific method) maintain that high-level abstractions, universals, "basic truths," and so on, do not exist except as names that are more or less useful. The realists (including the scholastics, Platonists, and many of those in the tradition of theology and metaphysics) argue that universals do indeed exist and are not "mere names." For a contemporary statement of a realist position, including an attack on the assumptions underlying this book, see Richard Weaver, *Ideas Have Consequences* (Chicago: Univ. of Chicago Press, 1947), Introduction and Chapters 1 and 8 especially.

and catalogues, advertising and postage stamps. Or you can include this "very thing" among the items classified by a word like *Americana*, so that this book obtains a status equal with hot dogs, aluminum lawn furniture, Civil War momentos, and McGovern buttons. More abstract still are words like *cultural artifact*, *object*, or *thing*.

We are sometimes not aware of how abstract our language is until it evokes some negative reaction from a person who hears it and who must respond to it. Try going to a drug store and say you want some medicine. Most likely the clerk will pause, waiting for you to be more specific. Or he might just laugh. Or question your sanity. Once I asked a clerk in a camera store if he bought used cameras. He said yes and asked what kind I wanted to sell. "It's a Retina," I replied, thinking that might be helpful. The clerk rolled his eyes upward and said, "How nice. I have a camera, too. It is a Kodak. Anything else?"

"Chinese food" sounds as if it is at a fairly low level abstraction, especially if you are deciding what kind of restaurant to go to. But once you go to a Chinese restaurant to order, "Chinese food" is hopelessly abstract.

Another way of thinking of levels of abstraction is to recall the strategies in the game of "Twenty Questions." The best strategy is to start with the most abstract possibilities first ("animal, vegetable, or mineral") and then slowly move to lower and lower levels of abstractions as the field is narrowed. Children who first learn the game don't realize this and sometimes guess a low level abstraction for the first question, "Is it Freddy's shoelaces?"

These remarks may make it appear that terms at lower levels of abstraction are always preferable to those at a higher level, or that higher level abstractions are more prejudicial than words that are more specific. This is not necessarily true, however. Take, for example, the move to add a word like "Ms." to the vocabulary. Many women argued that having only a choice between "Miss" or "Mrs." was unjust, for that required specifying the marital status of the woman; the use of "Mr." for men, however, was more abstract, making no indication of the man's marital status. The women may have a point. Certainly "Ms." is a convenient term, though if it is still used by a small percentage of women, it may serve more to identify their attitudes than anything else. Moreover, as we will note in the next chapter, we must not give language full credit for influencing our thinking in behavior. If it were only a matter of labels, Japanese society might appear to be the most sexually democratic in the world, since the label "*San*" is applied to both men and women, married or single. As anyone who is familiar with Japan knows, however, the symbolic distinctions between men and women in Japan are far more pronounced and rigid than anything found in the United States.

If you look at any sentence at random in this book or in your own discourse, you will probably find that the various words represent several levels of abstraction. When speaking or writing it is very difficult to maintain only one level of abstraction, be it high or low. Without such range we could not show any organization among things or indicate relationships. Also, speech that is consistently on only one level is dull and difficult to understand.

The caricature of a political speech is one bursting with highly abstract terms that may mean anything and therefore mean nothing: "Fellow Americans, let us face the future with humility, dedication, and a common purpose in the tradition of our forefathers. . . ." Democrat, Republican, radical, reactionary, Klansman, and socialist could affirm these words in unison. But when they become more specific the dissonance would thunder. And, of course, the social-political groups listed in the previous sentence are themselves highly abstract.

There are times to be specific and times to be abstract. Our friend, the child of a former example, might put up a sign on the family gate to warn visitors: "Beware of Dog." This is sufficient; he need not post the more specific notice "Beware of Spot." On the other hand, a visitor who saw the pet and asked, "What's your pet called?" would not be helped much if the child said "a dog." Knowing what the situation calls for determines how specific or how abstract one's speech must be. It is more difficult to know whether we are *responding* to words that stand for something rather specific in the sense-data world or words that represent so many possibilities that to give one response to all of them is foolish.

Usually, the farther we go from recognizable sense-data descriptions, the more misleading our statements and responses will be.

The distance from my once tipping a clerk at MacDonald's and "my basic generosity" is as far as Medea's passion is from "motherhood."

When we consciously manipulate our symbols for some gain (as when we apply for a job and describe having worked in a service station as having been "associated with the Petroleum Industry" or attempt to deduct from our taxes a visit to a massage parlor as "medical expense") we leap from level to level with amazing agility. We may regard these gymnastics as part of the game. But our gaming spirit is not present when we make the same leaps in the heat of prejudice or unthinking patriotism.

The idea of a vertical dimension in language (levels of abstraction) should not suggest that we can measure *specific* levels from one through twenty-five. We cannot. The idea of levels is merely a model or analogy to describe some of the differences among words. Relative to other terms we can say that a particular word is at a fairly low level, indicating rather specific conditions and qualifications of what is described. Or that a term is at a very high level of abstraction, so high that we can imagine a great many specifics that might be included in the term. But we cannot go through the dictionary and say that the first word is at the third level, the second word is at the fourteenth level, and the third word at the tenth level. Words are at our service and will be used differently by different people.

Science and Stereotypes. High-level abstractions may be useful or worthless, the result of the most careful kind of analysis or the result of the most careless. Prejudice and stereotyped reactions toward women, Italians, and farmers can exist only on the highest levels of abstraction—the individuals within any one class are utterly different. But before we damn high-level abstractions we should note that much that is important in the social and natural sciences is also at the highest level of abstraction. Scholars who are extremely careful about their observations of the world speak of "adolescents," "middle-income groups," "enzymes," and "pressure." The difference between the biologist and the bigot is not to be found in the presence or absence of high-level abstractions in their vocabularies, but rather in the original determination of those abstractions and in the attitudes toward them.

What is important is to know how high-level abstractions were obtained, what they mean, and thus to know what cautions may be exercised in using them. I find that six tests for evaluating high-level abstractions are very useful.

1. Is the term or statement involving the high-level abstraction *tentative or final?* The "laws" of science are like man-made laws in that they are made to be broken. A scientific "law," admittedly highly abstract, is tentative. When the law fails to account for what it claims to, it is disregarded and is replaced by another. When the person, be he scholar or average man, speaks with unswerving faith in his generalization he has abandoned the attitude of caution that characterizes the scientist at work.

2. Is the statement *absolute or probable?* Related to the previous test, this question reminds us that the words "never" and "always" do not appear in the vocabulary of the scientist. A statement like "children begin to talk at the age of ten months" means that *most* children do, or that your child *probably* will, and so on. It does not mean that all ten-month-olds conform to one "law." There is a problem, of course, in realizing that it makes little difference whether you say "women only want to get married" or "most women only want to get married"—the difference in attitude seems minor. But if words like "probably" or "tend to" or "often" were used in conversation more often, our conversations might be a little friendlier and we might be a little less demanding that the world conform to our laws.

3. Was the statement obtained inductively? In other words, how do you know what you say is true is true? Is this based on your experience? Only your experience? Or have others noted similar characteristics? The social desire to appear worldly or simply the need to make sense of the world often leads us to accept "fatherly advice" or "common-sense" statements at the higher levels of abstraction in place of careful observation at the level of experience. We must always ask how we came to know what we think we know.

4. Continuing with the previous test we must ask, can the high-level abstraction be applied to a specific case? If never or rarely, the "knowledge" is of little value. Although this question may seem to be obvious, there is much in poetry and platitude that occupies our thinking and conversation that has almost no application. Phrases like "truth is beauty, beauty truth," or "love makes the world go

'round" are common but almost impossible to apply. When the roommate or professor speaks only of principles and is unable to give an example we should be suspicious.

5. Can the high-level abstraction be applied to *everything*? If so, what does it tell us? In other words, does the abstraction add anything to what we already know? If not, then the comment is as useless as one that cannot be applied to anything. This test is basic to the scientific method. It is sometimes stated: given two alternative explanations or descriptions, the simpler one is to be preferred, and all that is unnecessary should be ignored. Dating to the classical dispute between realists and nominalists and named for William of Occam, this test is known as Occam's razor (shaving away the unnecessary) or the law of parsimony. In science the word *ether* was dropped from the vocabulary when it was discovered that no "ether" could be detected and that none was necessary for any explanation of the passage of light, the action of gravity, or any other effect. More common examples might include the phrases that begin "theoretically," for as often used, *everything* is "theoretically" possible. The words *God's will*, as they are often used mean nothing, for God's will can explain anything and therefore explains nothing.

6. Finally, does a specific abstract term exist as a useful invention or convenience, or is it regarded as a thing in itself? The term *reification* is used to describe the tendency to think that because there are certain words there must necessarily be certain "things" that correspond to them. To reify is to "thingify."

Even the social scientists have been prone to reify concepts of their own invention. Words like *ego, id, collective unconscious*, and so on are reified terms when the psychologist sets about to look for *things* that correspond to those *words*. If the term is a loose way of describing certain behavior, there is no problem. But if these inventions are thought to stand for real things, confusion can be the only result.

The problems with reification are especially common when the terms are preceded by adjectives like *real* or *pure* or *true* or *essential*. There is no such thing as "true love," there are only examples of feelings that might be called that in a moment of ecstasy. There is no "essential man," there are only men. And so on.

A Summary: Meaning Is As Meaning Does

Language is personal. Learned through imitating sounds that are associated with things, our language is our own, determined by the training, whims, and historical accidents of our culture, community, and family. To the extent that each person's associations and experiences are different, each person's language is a little different. Words of one speaker may sound very much like those of another. Object referents may be similar for many persons, but the experiences that determine the meaning (in response) can never be quite the same for any two people. If we recognize the arbitrary manner in which we have learned our language, we should be freer to change those semantic habits that, although they "made sense" to us as children, no longer seem sensible in light of additional experiences and increased understanding. Language is personal, but the "personality" of language should change as we do, and as our knowledge does.

What we call things is a matter of convention, determined by the culture in which we mature. Language requires us to divide our total experience into parts, each of which is given a name. That we need so few names to describe an infinite number of experiences demonstrates the remarkable economy of language, but at the same time it may confuse us into thinking that our experiences and perceptions are also composed of these separate elements that correspond to the language in which they are described. We must be careful not to confuse the necessity of linguistic distortion with the raw experience of the nonverbal world.

We have many choices of what to call things in a language. The exact words we use at a particular time reflect our attitudes and purposes at that time. What we consider important and what our society considers important will be given special attention through "special words"—often, many words for what another language would recognize in only one or two words.

However, because our language habits are so pervasive, there is a "feedback" effect through which we tend to perceive those things for which we have labels and ignore those for which we do not have labels. The perceptual efficiency of seeing the verbally delinieated object may also reduce the care with which we *look* at what we have labeled, with the result that we only "see the label" and not the thing. A person who is mature in his semantic habits will avoid being perceptually bound to his language and will attempt to see the world rather than read it.

Language, for each person, begins with naming, and for many persons, the ability to give names to things continues to be the mark of erudition. Semanticists have discouraged this overemphasis on naming things when the label becomes more important than the perception it denotes. The stage of giving names to things was called the "first dimension of language."

From the stage of naming "things," we moved to a second dimension of language, the sensitivity to different words on different levels of abstraction. Whereas some labels refer to rather specific sense data, other labels refer to abstractions of rather vague and general sense data. Our language structure offers us no clue to help us distinguish between the low-level abstractions and the higher-level abstractions, though this awareness of what we are talking about is obviously very important. If we react in similar ways to words on different levels of abstraction, our semantic behavior is confused. Sensitivity training for more discriminate reactions has been most important in the field of general semantics.

High-level abstraction, including generalizations, are extremely useful, for they help to show order and relationships. When the high-level abstractions may be clearly related to sense-data experience, these words are both convenient and important. Such high-level abstractions also characterize some language habits at their worst, for they are the basis for stereotypes and evocative terms that mean nothing because they might refer to anything. The thoughtful speaker is aware of the many things that might be designated by his words, and thus speaks with caution and qualification.

Because high-level abstractions include the most highly valued terms in our vocabulary (beauty, love, truth, justice, and so on) and because such words represent so many ambiguous but deep feelings, we may seek to objectify the terms. This behavior, reification, makes a thing of the label. With our map indicating only a word, we set out to search for a *thing*. When this happens we can only be disappointed or deluded. Put another way, instead of labeling an experience, we may attempt to experience a label.

FOUR
BUT WORDS CAN
NEVER HURT ME

As children we learn to chant that sticks and stones may break our bones but words can never hurt us. Some philosophers have said very much the same thing. Ludwig Wittgenstein, for one, said that the world is independent of our will—in our terms, the world is what it is regardless of what we call it. And so it is, the semanticist agrees, with some of this world but not with all of it. The division between natural science and social science might be the distinction between worlds unaffected by language and those that are very much changed by language. The brick may not care in the least whether it is called *a brick*, or *structural material*; but the brick layer may behave differently if he is called *laborer* or *artisan* or *construction engineer*. In the world of people, of conversation and argument, personal adjustment and insanity, words exert a tremendous influence.

In this chapter we shall apply and expand some of the principles presented earlier in order to illustrate a few of the many ways in which words influence behavior.

The Inherent Bias

No category is neutral. Not only does a classification reflect a purpose, but often an attitude is associated with the classification, too. If I were to tell you about a friend, Mr. Flores, your attitudes toward him might vary depending on whether I said he was a college senior, a mathematics major, a football player, a poet, or a Chicano. It is possible that my friend can be described in all of these terms —terms *not meant* to influence a response one way or another. But your attitude might be different with each different classification. Since the meaning of any label is partly in the listener, I have no idea of what my friend, Flores, might mean to you. You may like "football players" but dislike student "poets." You may think that all mathematics majors are brilliant but most Chicanos are better athletes than students. If so, clearly you are not talking about my friend Flores, you are talking about your responses to words.

Popular persuaders—speakers, advertisers, journalists, and so on—are well aware of the impact of classification. Where a person can anticipate a generally consistent response to a term, favorable or perjorative, such a classification may be emphasized. A Chicago newspaper, for example, used to use two sets of classifications for the same State senator: one if they were commenting on his actions that they approved and another set of classifications if they described his actions that they did not approve. (Incidentally, you should note your response to my classification of "State senator" in the previous sentence.) In one case the the Senator was the "Man - who - has - twice - won - the - best - legislator - award - by - the - Better Government - Association Senator." In another context he was the "member - of - the - pro-labor - left - wing - Independent - Voters - of Illinois Senator."

One of the popular propaganda devices is called *name calling*, and students sometimes are taught that this is a nasty practice. But all labeling is "name calling"—just as the choice of the word *propaganda* is a name (a name for what *they* do—*we* present only *information*). The tendency is to think that labels that cause unfavorable reactions are "name calling," but those that are favorable or those we habitually use are not. This is not true, of course. If we call Aaron Burr a traitor (which the court did not) and Washington a patriot, we are calling both names.

It is only when we think we have somehow totally characterized or "captured the essence" of the nonverbal world with a name that we run into difficulty. So long as we realize that no word does this and that any classification is but one of many possible, each with different attitudes and responses involved, we need not be deluded by language.

Some Words About Words About Words About . . .

Thus far we have discussed some of the ways in which words can distort our understanding of "things," even to the point of influencing changes in those things. Another problem that results from confusing word and thing is quite different. This is the problem that is sometimes caused by the self-reflexive nature of language. That is, we may make words about things, or words about *words* about things. In the second case we are one step removed from the first case. The problem is that unless the two kinds of relations (words-for-things and words-for-words-for-things) are distinguished we may begin to react to our own reactions.

Franklin Roosevelt's famous phrase, "We have nothing to fear but fear itself," is a warning of this kind of problem. It is one thing to be afraid, it is something else to be afraid of being afraid. The former may be healthy behavior, the latter a neurosis.

A common occurrence in introductory public speaking classes is the fear of speaking. It is natural for a speaker to be nervous. Few speakers ever completely lose this sensation when they first begin a speech; later, perhaps, most of the sensation of fear passes. But if a speaker is afraid of his becoming afraid, he will have much more difficulty in dealing with those tensions.

Other sensations a person feels, such as love, are natural, desirable, human. "Being in love" is one thing; "being in love with being in love" is something else. "Prejudice" is one thing; "prejudice of prejudice" is something else.

A statement that contains a reference to itself must be evaluated in a way that is different from a statement about something on the nonverbal level. This principle finds a parallel in the "theory of types," attributed to Bertrand Russell, which says that a class may not be a member of itself. Thus if I say, "There is an exception to every rule; this is a rule," I am including the statement itself in what it describes, and this creates an apparent paradox. Some of these may be amusing or entertaining puzzles to pass the time. But as the studies of interpersonal communication and psychological counseling have increasingly demonstrated in recent years, many of us employ comparable strategies for purposes that are anything but amusing. A patient tells his therapist, "Don't believe anything I tell you . . . I always lie." Is that also a lie? Or does that refer only to other subsequent utterances? Some persons (whom we might label as "sick") consciously turn their language upon itself to create confusions or paradoxes which they regard as protective. Language gives us this option.

The "That-Was-No-Lady" Syndrome

A well known framework for humor is to take one "thing" on the nonverbal level and then talk about it using two different but appropriate names that appear to be mutually exclusive. This is the basis for the classic line, "That was no lady, that was my wife," and for unintentional humor, as when one says, "He's not my friend, he's my brother." Shakespeare employed the same technique in *Henry IV*, Part I, where Falstaff swears off his thieving ways. "I must give over this life, and I will give it over," Falstaff states to his friends. When Hal immediately proposes another theft, Falstaff enthusiastically assents. Asked why the inconsistency, Falstaff answers, "Why, Hal, 'tis my vocation, Hal. 'Tis no sin for a man to labor in his vocation." In other words, "That was no sin, that was my vocation." Not all applications of the same principle result in humor.

Because any one "thing" may be classified in a variety of ways there need not be a necessary conflict between different classifications for this "same thing." Yet we frequently make problems for ourselves when we assume that differing classifications are mutually exclusive. When we ask whether a vacation should be relaxing or energetic, we may forget that it may be both at once. When we ask whether a work of literature should tell a good story or have a message, we may forget that the best of literature may have both. When we ask whether students should take a course for knowledge or for a good grade, we may forget that the two need not conflict. These apparent but unnecessary verbal conflicts that arise in discussions I call the "that-was-no-lady syndrome." They frequently begin as two valuable views of the same subject and conclude as nasty arguments in which each category threatens the other one. Somewhere the humor of it all is lost.

There are areas where different labels are, within a particular system, mutually exclusive. In law, for example, it is often necessary to select one label to the exclusion of another even if to an outsider both labels seem to apply. Is X a monopoly or merely efficient production? It may be both, but in the courtroom the distinction may be necessary. Is Y perjury or merely "lapse of memory"? To a disinterested party both may apply, but the prosecution and defense will take sides. Is Z premeditated murder or an act of mercy killing motivated by love? And so on. You can probably think of many examples in politics, in ethics, in marketing, in dating customs—in any field—where the rules, stated or assumed, encourage a choice to be made among descriptions that apply equally.

When one finds a conflict that can be stated in the familiar pattern *That was no———that was———*, having both words apply to the same nonverbal thing, he should ask why it is necessary to argue. One does much better to return to the nonverbal world for closer scrutiny than to haggle over two words.

This suggestion may seem to be a superficial and naïve approach to the solution of many of life's conflicts, and for some problems I am sure it is. If, however, you will take the trouble to apply the test of non-mutual-exclusion, I think that you will find that often it is useful. You may find, too, that the unnecessary verbal conflict is the more naïve attitude.

The Narrowed Vision

The previous discussion has dealt with terms that need not be mutually exclusive but which are treated as if they were. A still more common problem is the tendency to select mutually exclusive categories that are unnecessary in the first place. As soon as we select categories that are limited and extreme (at opposite poles) we are asking for trouble.

When our categories become narrowed, our perceptual world may become narrowed, too. This is most common and possibly most dangerous when we divide the world into only two categories—good or bad, right and wrong, black or white. Semanticists use the term *two-valued orientation* for this tendency, a term roughly equivalent to the *disjunctive fallacy* of classical logic. Korzybski believed that the two-valued orientation was encouraged by the second law of Aristotelian logic (the law of the excluded middle), which says that everything is either A or *not*-A. In some systems, the logic is valid and appropriate.[1] In everyday application, however, the dichotomy is not so practical.

Korzybski was highly critical of what he called the two-valued orientation and proposed instead that we maintain a multivalued orientation. A simple analogy may illustrate the difference. Compare the on–off switch of a radio or hi-fi set with the knob that controls the volume. With the former there are only two possibilities: either the set is on or it is off. But once it is on, the volume may be turned so low as to seem to be off, or it may be turned full blast. If there are a few people in the room, we might note, all will readily agree that the set is on or off. But they may disagree completely about just where to set the volume. This analogy may help to explain one reason the two-valued orientation is attractive in some cases for some persons: it makes choices and agreement apparently simpler. Unfortunately—or fortunately—the world seems more accurately and more richly described in terms of degrees and gradations.

[1] Some critics have argued that even for Aristotle's day, the two-valued logic was unnecessarily limiting. See Hans Reichenbach, *The Rise of Scientific Philosophy* (Berkeley: University of California Press, 1959), pp. 215–218.

Are there any events that have only two clear-cut possibilities? Life and death used to seem like the most obvious examples, even though Eastern philosophers have traditionally argued that these were not at all opposites but rather part of the same reality. In many cases, of course, there is no disputing that this person is alive and that body is dead. But there are some cases where the change is not so clear, and far from being a mere semantic problem, the issue can involve interpretations from biology, medicine, law, and ethics. Only a few years ago there was common agreement that one was dead when the person's heart stopped beating. Now, of course, it is possible to revive once-stilled hearts or even to transplant hearts. Thus the brain has come to be the criterial organ in determining death for many doctors and according to some laws. At this point, however, it is possible for a person to be "alive," according to some criteria, and "dead" according to others.

Are there other events which are appropriately symbolized as either/or, two-valued alternatives? Are there other events which cannot accurately be described as more or less, to some degree, a little bit, or mostly? Can the girl be a little bit pregnant? There are situations in which one makes a choice to do something or not to do something—to find the plaintiff guilty or not guilty (though this is clearly the application of a label to a very complex nonverbal event), to marry or not to marry (and, of course, here there are marvelous compromises, too).

During times of stress and great tension, the number of possible responses is reduced. As we tend toward signal reactions we may reduce the choices to two—"you are either for me or ag'in' me," "you are either an American or an un-American," "you will either be saved or be damned." Popular persuaders of all kinds—politicians, ministers, advertisers, (Mother?)—all have found it effective to narrow a choice to one of two alternatives. Most often the language of the proffered alternatives leaves little choice. In a syndicated column that appeared under the by-line of Senator Barry Goldwater, the choices to the question "How do you stand?" have included these:[2]

---

[2] Quoted by Fred J. Cook, *Barry Goldwater: Extremist of the Right* (New York: Grove Press, 1964), p. 113.

"How do you stand, sir?—for voluntarism or compulsion?" "How do you stand, sir?—for maximum opportunity or for a stereotyped, carbon-copy society?" "How do you stand, sir?—for liberty or for slavery?"

Certain mental aberrations have been described in terms of the two-valued orientation—the paranoiac who evaluates his world in terms of threats or nonthreats, for example. In his fine book, *People in Quandaries*, Wendell Johnson[3] presents the argument that many mental disturbances can be traced to semantic disorientations. Johnson believes that many serious problems are reflected in the two-valued orientation. Healthy people, he argues, are more comfortable with many classifications for acts and other people, whereas the disturbed person is happiest when he has only to choose between two possibilities.

Some of Johnson's conclusions have been challenged.[4] The authors state that "If anything, results suggest that normals are more comfortable in the neat dichotomies than are neurotics." Because different approaches were used in the studies, there is no need to support one view or the other. There are neurotic tendencies to be squeamish about making any decision, and there are defensive tendencies in which outsiders are classified as threatening or nonthreatening. Moreover, the distinction between "normal" and "disturbed" persons is deceptively two-valued.

It is sufficient to recognize that any verbal system is arbitrary and that no matter how many ways we slice up the world we are still distorting it. But to limit the number of just two possibilities is extremely distorting and is a semantic problem to be avoided if at all possible.

Caught in the Act

It is a characteristic of the English language, among others, that although our verbs have specific tenses, our nouns rarely offer

[3] Wendell Johnson, *People in Quandaries* (New York: Harper and Brothers, 1946), p. 294–335.

[4] (Charles E. Osgood, George J. Suci, Percy H. Tannenbaum, *The Measurement of Meaning* (Urbana: University of Illinois Press, 1957), p. 250.

temporal clues. Thus, we can use different tenses of the verb *to go* and say "the boy goes," or "the boy will go," or "the boy went," but we cannot easily construct a sentence that would include all of those possibilities. However, with a noun, like *boy*, the opposite is true. There is nothing in a noun (or adjective) that indicates its position in time and space. Although there is an obvious convenience to such indefinite, all-time nouns, they may also present us with many problems if we are not careful.

If I write about Roman Catholics or Republicans or fraternities, I apparently must include all that has been classified under these labels. I may, if I choose, add additional words of qualification—"the Roman Catholics in Spain, 1503" or "the Roman Catholics at the Second Ecumenical Council"—which make the term a little more specific. A sampling of daily conversation would probably indicate that we prefer to speak of mass-nouns and adjectives rather than take the trouble to be more specific.

Korzybski suggested that we add subscripts to our terms that would remind us of differences among events denoted by a vague noun. Thus, we should not speak of Republican policies, but rather of Republican policies $_{1872}$ and Republican policies $_{1972}$; not of "the free-enterprise system," but of "free enterprise $_{Railroad\ Industry,\ 1883}$" and "free enterprise $_{Yin\ Yang\ Chop\ Suey\ House,\ 1975}$." Although such notations may not do much for one's turgid prose style, they may do a great deal for clarity of expression.

Instead of thinking of yourself as "me," it is wiser to indicate different "me's" for different years and in different situations. This might call attention to the obvious fact of change and growth matters that are significant but often obscured under the label "me." It is popularly believed that each person has something of an "essence" or "core" that never changes and is the "basic person" or the "authentic person." I am not sure that this is a very realistic view for a lifetime, though our language habits certainly encourage the attitude. It can be argued that an individual at any particular time in his life shares more characteristics with others of his age and background than he does with "himself" from the cradle to the grave. Indeed it is this commonality that permits meaningful studies in human behavior. The point here is not that we change our names periodically to mark our growth and behavioral change, but merely that we remember that there is much change that can be concealed in one name for "one thing."

Very closely related to this tendency to conceptualize "things" indefinitely is the habit of verbally extending a single event into a pervasive characteristic. There is a difference between saying "Arthur lied to me last Tuesday," and saying "Arthur is a liar." Many persons utter sentences of the second kind when the more accurate statement would be the first one. Or take this pair of sentences: "Louie murdered his aunt last September" and "Louie is a murderer." Here the confusion between the two is still more common, as a glance at the morning paper might show. Some people might reason, "Of course we all lie now and then but that doesn't make us *liars*; but once you murder somebody you definitely *are* a murderer." And yet the principle of extending a single event to a total description is the same in both cases. It is just that we have stronger feelings about murder than we do about lying.

Using generalized labels saves time and effort and also makes us appear to "know more." In the process, of course, our thinking and communication is clearly distorted. What is worse, such labels often stick and even become the basis for other inferences that compound the distortion. We may avoid the subtle dangers of generalized labels if we take the trouble to be more specific and state the conditions under which the label is applied.

Living Up to the Label

We may carry the previous discussion two steps further, in this section and the next, and observe that in some cases such labels can bring about changes in the nonverbal world. Words intended as descriptions-only become instrumental in changing what they describe.

The attitude of "one-thing–one-label" is especially problematic then the label refers to us. We have a tendency to live up to our labels, whether those labels have been applied by others (clown, party girl, brain, and so on) or those we have chosen for ourselves (clown, party girl, brain, and so on). Wendell Johnson wrote extensively on the problem of stuttering, believing that persons become stutterers only after they have been called "stutterer." By being given a name that calls attention to an otherwise temporary speech difficulty ("I think our Johnny is a stutterer"), the child becomes curious, begins to respond to the new label, and in his responses he "becomes a stutterer." Without a word to give significance to his behavior, it is possible Johnny would not have continued to have such problems.

Often there is comfort in responding to a label. You may prefer to say "I am a Libra or "I am a chess freak," than to have no such label at all. If you label yourself as "no good in math" or "a lousy public speaker" or "the quiet type," you may continue to prove that this is so. Responding to such labels gives us direction, even if the direction is backwards; responding to such labels helps us decide what to do and what not to do, even if the choices are not the wisest. In such behavior we fail to recall the circumstances under which the label was first applied and the degree to which our interpretation of the situation determined our choice of label.[5]

There is a social convenience in living up to labels, too, for to some degree society's labels indicate prescribed roles and the "rules of the game" of the culture. Some of the accepted social differences between the sexes might be explained in this way. "Martha won't try to repair anything because, after all, she's a *woman*." And "John will be blunt and businesslike because, after all, he's a *man*." That each sex accepts the mythologies of the other brings about a convenient division of labor or a sometimes unfunny battle of the sexes. The change in behavior of women during this century began when great numbers decided that they did not have to live up to the social meaning of the label *woman*. The change will be complete only when men accept the change in meaning, too.

[5] For a vital theory of personality related to the tendency to live up to labels, see Carl Rogers, *Client-Centered Therapy* (Boston: Houghton Mifflin, 1951), pp. 481–533.

Saying It May Make It So

It is clear that when one tries to live up to a label he has given himself, he limits his activities to those the label has prescribed. It is possible, however, for persons to change the character of behavior of other persons and institutions by labeling them and then by acting on the label.

Suppose, for example, you label the students on your campus as "unfriendly." Having decided that the students are unfriendly, you begin to treat them as if they *were* unfriendly—avoiding opportunities to talk, not smiling when you pass them, and so on. The result will be that those students whom you often see will recall that you didn't smile or talk, and may then begin to behave in an unfriendly manner toward you. If enough other students also label those around them as "unfriendly," the result *will be* an unfriendly campus. If you are about to enter a discussion, and you think "this discussion will be dull and unprofitable," the appropriate way to act on your description is to take little part in the discussion. If others describe the situation as you do, the discussion *will be* dull and unprofitable.

This common language habit has been called "the self-fulfilling prophecy" by sociologist Robert K. Merton. When we predict that something of which we are a part will happen, our prediction may be instrumental in *causing* that something to happen. Not only statements directly involving the speaker ("I think we shall never be married, dear") but also statements which indirectly involve the speaker may take the form of the self-fulfilling prophecy. If the admissions director of a private school believes (predicts) that "Jews are aggressive and work too hard, compared to our other students," he may urge that a quota be set limiting the number of Jewish students to be admitted. If there is such a quota and you, a bright Jewish student, know it, what must you do to be among the college's "chosen people?" You might have to be somewhat aggressive and work extra hard. (There, you see!) If a company president believes that Black employees just don't work as hard as his white employees, what kind of jobs and with what expectations will the company offer prospective Black employees? Probably jobs that require less responsibility, less work—and the kind that will be the first to be "laid off." And if you are Black and given such a job, what kind of work will you feel like doing?

If your government is sure that the government across the border will take advantage of any weakness in your country and launch an attack at any time, what kind of military posture should your country present? Troops may be sent to the border, warning speeches may be made, and so on—almost any newspaper will provide other details of current examples. Given that, what kind of reaction is likely from the enemy? Often the response is one that seems to prove your government's first prediction.

It would be naive to explain the causes of religious or racial bigotry, or the international arms race and wars, simply in terms of this pattern. But the self-fulfilling prophecy surely contributes to the cause and the perpetuation of such events.

Note that the self-fulfilling prophecy works only when the area about which the prediction is made may, in some way, be acted upon. It does not apply to statements like "It must not rain tomorrow" or any other descriptions or predictions that are not socially based.

Blame It on the Language

"Black is beautiful," proclaimed the slogan during a period of civil rights activism, "Black power" advocacy, and general Black consciousness-raising. In addition to evoking ethnic pride (and some ethnocentric fear), the slogan also attempted to counteract a pattern in American English language habits in which "black" is consistently used with negative associations. We speak of "blackmail," and "the black sheep of the family," and some groups exclude members by "blackballing" them. We attach "black" to the day on which disaster falls, "Black Monday," etc. The evil man is said to have a "black heart" or a "black soul." It is very difficult to think of "black" in figures of speech where the meaning is positive or even neutral. Not only the word "black" but the color symbolism as well is often used for similar purposes: the bad guys in old Westerns wear black hats and often ride black horses, and villains most often had black hair. Black is the symbol of mourning in this part of the world and the color of the hearse. Many people have argued that such language and other symbolic habits provide a semantic bias toward people with "black skin," and thus such usage abets, if not actually causes, racial conflicts. If black and white are the conventional opposites, symbolically, why not expect an inevitable conflict between black men and white men?

When the women's movement emerged a few years later, a similar semantic attack was launched on the male bias in our language habits. Some traced this bias as far back as the symbolic personification of the deity as male (God the father); others assailed the generic "man" in our language: mankind, workman, chairman, and so on. Some of the critics have demanded that such words be replaced with more neutral words or sexless affixes: "people" for "mankind," "worker" for "workman," "chairperson" for "chairman," and so forth. In mixed company, everybody watches his or her language.

But does it matter? Do such language habits really bias our thinking? Do we really make the transfer from "blackmail" and the other black symbolism to skin color. (Indeed, do we really perceive skin as being black or being white?) Are the seeds of male chauvinism sown in the language? The patterns are there, surely, and one can note the correlations. But does blaming the language go to the source of the problem, and will changing the language change social behavior? Before considering an answer, let us consider another possible discriminatory bias in our language habits.

If we look at the directional "left" and "right" in English, we also find words that are often paired for negative and positive associations. A "right-hand man" is helpful,[6] a "left-handed compliment" is practically an insult. In our borrowing from French, one who is "adroit" (meaning "right") is skillful; the clumsy one is "gouche" (meaning "left"). Even the homonyms, those words which sound the same but have different meanings (though some are derived

[6] A right-hand woman is also helpful, of course.

from the directional words) follow the same pattern: it is better to be right (not "wrong"), to claim your rights, and to affirm your agreement ("right on!") than to be left—left alone or left out in left field. Do we have here the beginnings of a "Left-handed People's Liberation Movement?" Therefore, why not "Child Power," since many expressions using the words "child" or "children" applied to adults insult children: being "childish," "mere child's play," etc.

Perhaps the underlying pattern in all of these cases is a two-valued, good-bad logic which is symbolized in terms that have traditionally been regarded as natural opposites: black and white, male and female, right and left, and so on. While the black–white semantics probably does not help race relations, its usage antedates racial conflicts as they exist in the United States and, indeed, also is found in languages in parts of the world which are predominantly "black" and where there is relatively little racial discrimination. Sometimes our language habits do cause harm, as we have tried to show throughout this book. Sometimes blaming language habits is a rhetorically effective way to alert us to and dramatize a social problem. But also, sometimes attempting to change some conventional habits is not very effective in changing the attitudes and behavior which are at fault. We must be careful that our efforts are not misguided and wasted. Otherwise we will have achieved only a kind of "symbolic strategy," the topic which we will look at next.

Symbolic Strategies

It was the literary and rhetorical critic Kenneth Burke who gave the name *symbolic strategies* to the ways in which we may manipulate our symbols in lieu of altering reality. In one sense all of language and thought is a strategy for coming to symbolic terms with that muddled world of process and change. Every time we impose order on the outside world through language, we are applying some kind of strategy. Apart from the overall function of language, there are some special strategies, peculiar and often personal, by which we come to grips with things. We will consider four of these.

Possess the Symbol. One form of symbolic strategy is the apprehension of symbols when what the symbols represent is difficult or nearly impossible to obtain. Our mass society today can supply the symbols of almost everything to almost anybody with a few dollars to spend. Symbols of power, love, status, sex, and even humility may be represented in cars, pins, homes, magazines, or clothing.

Every year thousands of books on such varied subjects as winning friends, effective speaking, writing for profit, improving your memory, and learning hypnotism, are sold to persons who will never try to develop these skills. It is enough for these people to study the symbols of the skills. For most of us some of the time to "have that knowledge," which means *owning* some great books, knowing some special words, or having taken "that course," is our way of dealing with what those symbols represent.

Fool Thyself. We probably all know people who make it a habit to set their clocks and watches five or ten minutes ahead of standardized time. Such persons usually claim that this manipulation always gives them the extra few minutes they need when their clocks show them to be a little bit late. The logic of this self-deception is not altogether clear to me, but apparently it works for some people. It is another kind of symbolic strategy. Or take the example of students who have taken examinations but who have not yet received their grades. It is not uncommon for the students to tell themselves that they did more poorly than they "really think" they did. By fooling themselves in this way, the students believe they cannot be disappointed when the grades are announced.

Such symbolic strategies are not necessarily harmful because the deceptions are intentional and directed only to the individual. There may be elements of superstition or even ritual involved in such habits, too, but the underlying principle is to manipulate symbols in order to fool oneself in some vaguely useful or protective way.

Identification. Another variety of these symbolic strategies is the temporary identification with other persons who seem to have things under control. When we enjoy a "western" movie because it depicts a world in which the lines are clearly drawn between good and bad, right and wrong; we are entering symbolically a world that is more manageable than our own. We need only identify with the man-in-control to feel more important and more responsible. Such identification frequently lasts for some time after the program, film, book, or other vicarious experience, has ended. It is probably no accident that Westerns became adult fare on television during a time when the "real world" of the news reports was becoming increasingly confused. To find a world that we can deal with, we may escape to fantasies, biographies of famous people, or various melodramas. Much of the popular evocative rhetoric, in political speeches, sermons, commencement-day addresses, and the like, may serve the same function.

Mittyism. Instead of turning to the symbols produced for our identification by professionals, we may create our own fantasies. We have our choice of becoming a giant in a world of midgets, or of remaining ourselves and cutting the world down to our size. Thurber's Walter Mitty is a famous example of the former approach, though what Thurber depicted is by no means limited to fiction. Much of our sleeping activity, dreaming, appears to be normal and necessary to symbolically reestablish our position in the world. Such unconscious symbolic activity begins at a very early age. There is speculation, for example, that some young children who wet their beds are symbolically trying to drown their parents, an act that out-Mittys Mitty. In more familiar and conscious form is the employee who, among his coworkers, pokes fun at his boss because he cannot physically poke his boss. Other similar symbolic strategies go under the names of ridicule, sarcasm, and many kinds of jokes.

In order to give importance to ourselves and our petty problems we may prefer to remain as we are but involve the whole world with our problems. On the day of a difficult final examination, for example, you may think, "Maybe the college will burn down so I won't have to take it." Although this approach may seem more perverse and more cowardly, it may be no less common. Either way—to inflate yourself to be bigger than the big awful world, or to bring the world down to your size—the principle of manipulating symbols to deal with reality is in effect.

When we manipulate our symbols in order to deal with the world in a way that is comforting to us we are not necessarily acting in an unhealthy manner. For catharsis, for a boost in morale, or for a first step toward action, such strategies may be as healthy as they are common. But when we feel that we have altered something in the nonverbal world when we have only played with symbols; or when we escape to symbols so often that we cannot face up to the real problems; or when we confuse our imaginative world with what passes for the real world, we may find ourselves in serious trouble.

Sticks and stones may break our bones but words can never hurt us. Would that it were true. Injuries from sticks and stones can be repaired—or, if not, then at least we can collect on the insurance. The harm that words can cause is more subtle and sometimes more permanent. And, except in rare cases, there is no insurance policy that can even acknowledge the semantic damage. Moreover, it is the odd person who abuses himself with sticks or stones, but rare is the individual who does not suffer from some self-afflicted semantic wounds.

In this chapter we have reviewed some of the problems we create through language, and issued some general warnings and suggestions. Let the thinker beware. But let him not therefore stop thinking and speaking.

FIVE

ORGANIZING
OUR EXPERIENCE

Remember that great year at Plainfield State Teachers' College when the football team chalked up so many victories that it was ranked nationally among the top small college teams that were untied and undefeated? Remember the team's great quarterback, Johnny Chung, who would down a bowl of rice between the halves and come out to lead Plainfield on to victory and an invitation to the coveted Blackboard Bowl? No? Maybe you are too young to remember, for it was over thirty years ago when Plainfield State was part of the Saturday night football results. And just as well, too, because there was no such college as Plainfield State. It was all a hoax, later described by Alexander Klein in *Grand Deception*, devised by a New Jersey public relations man who was overwhelmed by the Saturday night litany of football scores which seemed to come mostly from places he'd never been and didn't really care to know about. The Plainfield eleven would have gone on to that glorious Blackboard Bowl, too, if *Time* magazine hadn't wanted to do a story on the team and their fabled quarterback Chung. Caught at last, the final news release described how the team, including Johnny, was all caught cheating on an exam, and the ball game was over.

Most of what we read about or hear about on radio or television concerns people we've never seen, places we've never visited, and events that may or may not ever happen. In the sports stories that year, Plainfield State Teacher's College of Plainfield, New Jersey, had as much symbolic reality as Notre Dame or Slippery Rock. It wasn't until somebody checked up that they found that there was no such school, that it was all a hoax. If that amuses you and you feel better for knowing about it, how do you know that this story and Alexander Klein and all that is not yet another hoax?

In this chapter we are not interested in the intentionally distorted expressions—like hoaxes, exaggerations, or lies (another interesting example of labeling)—but rather with the well-intentioned, most common statements we make and hear every day. We would like to be able to set forth some standards or criteria for evaluating what we say on the basis of its reliability, to be able to know *how* we know what we're talking about. We would like to allow for all kinds of expressions and yet be able to discriminate among them: to know the difference, for example, between what some would call "a fact" and what some would call "a hunch;" and between what nobody can dispute because it is your own personal judgment and statements that almost all of us agree on because, without knowing it, we have already agreed to agree.

We will begin with what seems to be a basic distinction.

A Double Standard: Sense Data and System

It is important to distinguish between two procedures for evaluating symbols: (1) the testing of a symbol against the nonverbal *sense-data reality*; and (2) the testing of a symbol within a *system of other symbols*. The sentence "Does this dog have fleas?" may be answered by examining the nonverbal dog. The sentence, "Does this dog have a soul?" may be answered, not by examining the dog, but by studying the way in which the word *soul* is used within some religious system. To examine the dog to discover his soul or to discuss in the abstract a question like "Does this dog have fleas?" is to confuse the two standards and thus to render any decision meaningless. When we fail to recognize that words may be tested against either standard, or when we confuse the two in the process of evaluation, our thinking will be confused.

These two standards for evaluation provide the two basic traditions and methods in philosophy and science, as well as in everyday behavior. There is a "sense-data orientation" (at the lowest levels of abstraction and often called the "extensional orientation" in the semantics of Korzybski), and there is a "system orientation" (at the higher levels of abstraction, with or without an awareness of the process of abstracting, and sometimes called by the semanticists an "intensional orientation.") In reasoning, the inductive method begins with the sense data and moves toward a systemization of it; the deductive method begins with the system and draws conclusions about sense data from the rules of the system.

We find the contrasting orientations of "sense data" emphasis *vs.* an emphasis on systems to be a convenient way to compare competing trends in the varied fields of education, philosophy, political theory, religion, and others. The "classical education" in the western world, for example, for centuries stressed "the seven liberal arts." Modern "liberal arts colleges" have long since strayed from the original seven disciplines, of course. But those original seven (rhetoric, grammar, logic, mathematics, geometry, music, and astronomy) were severely system oriented. All were concerned with learning the rules of the systems; the first three, the *Trivium*, were primarily verbal systems, the latter four, the *Quadrivium*, were primarily numerical. Astronomy was the only subject that sounds "scientific," but by studying the stars and planets—instead of plants and animals—one was seeking to discover the "eternal system" of a reality safely distant from the prying hands of curious students. More contemporary fields in education—the natural and social sciences, field studies, etc., are, in contrast, for more sense-data oriented.

Deductive reasoning, formal logic, mathematics, and a prescriptive approach to human behavior, including language, is primarily system oriented. Induction, empiricism, pragmatism, and a descriptive approach to human behavior (how people do act and talk, not how the rules say people should) is more sense-data oriented. Similarly, the distinction between conservative philosophies in religion and politics, with an emphasis on retaining the traditional social or moral order, leans toward the system side. Liberalism in its many forms in religion or politics or whatever stresses change, process, and challenges to "the system."

An obvious parallel exists between the two orientations of "sense data" and "systems" in the relationship of perceived "reality" and language. No two things in the world, it is said, are exactly alike: this is the lesson of the snowflakes. But we use the same words, over and over, for identifying things that are not really identical. Would it be possible to imagine a language where every word was different in order, in some way, to symbolize the awareness of the differences of things? The answer seems to be *no*. If every utterance were unique we would have no basis for imitating and hence learning a language and no basis for comprehension. In short, we would have no *system*, no language.

In the history of philosophy we find many thinkers who have emphasized the "system orientation" and others who have emphasized the sense-data orientation." F. S. C. Northrop[1] has suggested that the former has characterized Western thought and that the latter has characterized Eastern thought. Even Northrop's distinction might be regarded by some "Eastern philosophers" as essentially "Western," since it is so neatly two-valued (but maybe most would agree with him anyway).

But we do not have to pit West against East to illustrate the basic difference. Western philosophy has had its share of thinkers who have emphasized the "system orientation" and those who have emphasized "sense data." This is particularly true in the Anglo-American tradition, for much as Americans may pay homage to the genius of ancient Greece, American thought owes more to England and a very different empirical tradition. For purposes of illustration and simplification, consider the alternative philosophies of Plato and of Francis Bacon, the last of the Rennaisance men and the first of "the moderns."

Plato distrusted sense data because it was fleeting, differed from person to person, and was therefore unsound. His desire for something so permanent that it was eternal, unchanging, and everywhere the same represents what is sometimes called "the classical

[1] F. S. C. Northrop, *The Meeting of East and West* (New York: Macmillan, 1946).

attitude." In his *Theatetus*, for example, he presents what might have been a description of transactional perception such as was presented in the previous chapter of this book. However, instead of making the point that people see things differently, Plato makes the point that *because* perception is so complex, we must distrust it. For something more reliable, Plato moved to a system that was not of this world of senses, but of an "ideal" world where such problems did not exist. A Platonist of this century, Richard Weaver,[2] states the position clearly:

> Naturally, everything depends on what we mean by knowledge. I shall adhere to the classic proposition that there is no knowledge at the level of sensation, that therefore knowledge is of universals, and that whatever we know as a truth enables us to predict. The process of learning involves interpretation, and the fewer particulars we require in order to arrive at our generalization, the more apt pupils we are in the school of wisdom.
>
> The whole tendency of modern thought, one might say its whole moral impulse, is to keep the individual busy with endless induction. Since the time of Bacon the world has been running away from, rather than toward, first principles, so that, on the verbal level, we see "fact" substituted for "truth," and on the philosophical level, we witness attack upon abstract ideas and speculative inquiry.

Such a view may be comforting, but it binds us to other symbolic systems. Weaver, like Plato we might assume, is extremely distrustful of our attempts to appraise what we call "reality." (Reality is at the sense-data level, where triangles are never quite perfect, circles never exactly round, and descriptions at best only approximate expectations based on theory.) In short, the system orientation which we have tried to illustrate through Plato and a modern-day Platonist, Weaver, regards human perception of sense data as failing the elegance and consistency possible only in some symbolic system.

Francis Bacon represents the opposite view. His writings, which in so many ways anticipated by four hundred years the ideas of contemporary semanticists, reveal a nearly total distrust of "sys-

---

[2] Richard Weaver, *Ideas Have Consequences* (Chicago: University of Chicago Press, 1948, 1960), pp. 12–13.

tems" and an equally total faith in sense data. Bacon argued for "pure induction," by which he meant the careful cataloguing of sense data until one had a sufficient sampling of examples to move to something more general. The system would grow naturally but slowly. Before we could formulate a theory of "heat" or "light," for example, we would have to take all known instances of "heat" or "light" and study them. And then we could begin to generalize, to elaborate a system.

Neither view is satisfactory. A system that would disregard our daily experiences is of limited utility. And besides, we should ask where such a system came from before we accept it. [3] A system based purely on inducted sense data is impossible, for before we can use the terms *heat* or *light* we have to assume that they belong to some "system." What do we include and what do we exclude, we should ask? In both systems we find the ignorance of language as a human invention that has evolved through accident and convention, not design.

The way we interpret everyday experiences and the tradition of the scientific method both require combinations of system and sense data. To begin with incidents in our personal lives we may say that we have few "experiences" that do not involve, in different degrees, both sense data and an accepted system. By *experience* I mean all of the attitudes, anticipations, and so on, that come into play whenever we perceive something. To take a pleasant example, a kiss is something more than sense data. If one reflects on the event, as persons have been known to do, what one means when he or she says "I have been kissed" is not just the recollection of tactile senses, but something much more complex. It is an experience that involves the system in which a kiss has some significance (love or respect or betrayal) but something that is not *just* some verbal classification of the meaning of a kiss.

Or, if one observes that "it is raining," his experience is not just sense data. If it were, his description would be completely different when he was inside looking out from what it would be if he were standing in the rain. The sense data are different in each case.

[3] Often the explanation of total systems is that they are "inspired" and therefore preferable to our own homely ideas.

Inside, he could see something, he might hear something, he might smell something. Outside, he might feel something, he might smell something, he might or might not see something. Why call both by the same name *rain*? To observe that "it is raining" is an interpretation that goes beyond any sense data, for the idea of "rain" is part of a system that has organized a whole constellation of experiences into the classification *rain*.

It is difficult to pass a day and maintain a totally "sense-data orientation" or a totally "system orientation." As we try to make our experiences meaningful we move from one orientation to the other. Nor, of course, are the two positions as neat and fixed as this discussion might indicate.

The attitude of the semanticist tends to distrust verbal systems that would limit our experience or alter the nonverbal world to fit the verbal world. Life experiences should be served by language, and not the other way around. To this extent (and in this direction) the semanticist is sense-data oriented.

To summarize for now, let us say that all experience is a combination of immediate sense data that is given meaning within a larger system. The system may be the system of language by which we determine and classify some event. Or the system may be religious or political or social, by which we interpret the event. In the first case, it is cultural and linguistic and unavoidable; in the second, it is more personal and, to some extent, a matter of choice. With sense data only, we can go nowhere (if indeed we can have "sense data only" when we grow up in a society and learn a language before we are conscious of it). With system only, we are hyperinterpretive, overly linguistic, or "hung up on words and systems." What is important is the point at which we begin and emphasize. The directives provided by the previous chapter indicate that we are safer if we start with the *experience*, as close to the sense data as we can be.

Mature and Premature Organization of Experience

Every day we have occasion to place events into some system that seems to work for us. If it is a cold winter morning and the car doesn't start the first time or the second time or the third time, we must decide whether it will start the fourth time (or nth time) or whether we should take the bus. At the time of the decision we trust a system based on past experiences. We move from the extensional experience to the intensional interpretation ("Eventually this car will start" or "This car will never start"). When to do this is unpredictable. Or, it is predictable only within a range of probability. If you were totally "system oriented" you would know what would happen before you tried. If you were purely inductive you would never quite know.

Often, we make judgments of other people on the basis of the *results* of their systems or lack of them. "Some people don't know when to quit," we say of the fool. "Some people have what it takes," we say of the hero. Now, the fool and the hero may be the same person—but the hero has tried one more time.

Greek mythology is filled with characters who are extravagantly extensional, though more through punishment than compulsion or fortitude.[4] Sisyphus and Tantalus come to mind immediately. Their efforts are still continuing, so far as we know. We may feel hope or pity or, since Camus, *et al.*, identification toward them. If we are "in on the mythology," we know that the fruits and drink for Tantalus will always be just out of reach, and that Sisyphus never had a chance, either. But we can say this only about "others," for it is their choice, not ours, whether or not to try again, whether or not to make a general conclusion (a system). When it is our choice we know that we don't know for sure. We tend to act in predictable behavior, it is true, not because anything is inevitable but because, in classical terms, we become products of our own mythology. In this sense, the faithful who never gives up and the neurotic who always gives up are not so different except in the label we give them. Our own lives are spent in that vast land in between.

There are many instances in which our prediction of what will

---

[4] This is one explanation for classical Greek punishment. As in Greek tragedy, the idea of inevitability (system) is crucial in the cruel Greek punishment. Perhaps in our day in which probability, not certainty, is the rule, our attitude toward the punishment is different.

happen (our classification of some experience into a system) is influential in determining what does happen. Such instances we discussed in Chapter 4. But to the extent that "the world is independent of our will" we have to make guesses. What guesses we make will depend, in part, on how we describe "the world" in the first place.

Ordinary Language

In order to record or communicate our experiences, we reduce those experiences to symbols that can be popularly understood. Because these symbols must be negotiable within the whole society that speaks our language, our symbolic expressions of experiences are necessarily "loose," even sloppy. Language is never precise, for its very nature and purpose require it to be more general than any single experience that might be described in the language. This "ordinary language" conveys the bulk of our symbolized experience. A scientist or specialist in any field demands a more precise language, for those who read or hear his words are a smaller population with special training in the language.

Moreover, since language is a product of man, there is something of man in all of his statements—even those that seem to be statements about the "outside world." As we noted before, when one moves from sense data to experience, the degree of personal involvement increases considerably, and most of our meaningful expressions are about "experiences" of one kind or another. There are degrees of personal involvement in statements about the "outside world," however. The enthusiastic drunk who praises his performing elephants or the child who complains to his parents about the billion tigers in his bedroom or the D student who stands in the rain looking at his first A paper and exclaims that "it is a beautiful day!" are very much a part of what they presume to describe. But though these examples are extreme, the difference is one of degree. Whenever we say anything we put something of us into what we describe. Even though our ordinary language is less than precise, we can still make important distinctions among kinds of sentences.

These provide standards for evaluation that are very important if we are to use our language as best we can. For example, we may distinguish among the following sentences:

1. *The dog is barking.*
2. *The dog is healthy.*
3. *The dog is man's best friend.*
4. *The "dog" is a four-legged animal that barks.*

All of the above sentences begin with the same three words. All use a common subject, *the dog*, followed by the ubiquitous and, in English, ambiguous verb *is*. And yet, each sentence, if we imagine a probable context, is different. The first is a sentence of description, the second is a sentence based on inference, the third is a value judgment, and the fourth is a tautology. These four sentence types probably encompass most of our ordinary conversation. We shall examine these one at a time.

Statements of Description

If we have a dog before us and the dog is barking, we should be able to agree on the statement, "The dog is barking." If we were all deaf, we might be able to see the dog open and close its mouth but not tell whether the dog was barking or not. ("I see it open and close its mouth, but I hear nothing—is it barking?") As the word *barking* is usually used, it refers to sound. To make a statement about sound we must be capable of perceiving such sound.

Likewise, if we could not observe the dog, we would have no basis for our agreement. Suppose, for example, we know from experience that when the phone rings in Barney's apartment, his dog barks wildly. Our idea of a good time is to telephone Barney's apartment and know that his dog will begin barking when the phone rings. We may agree that Barney's dog is barking when we telephone, but because we cannot *observe* the dog our agreement may not be justified.

The most accurate statements are those made about the observed by persons capable of observation. Because of the limitations of any single individual, the more persons who can observe and agree about their observations, the more trust we can put into their common statements of description. Agreement alone is not a sufficient criterion for putting trust into a statement. There are many ways of producing agreement in society, from the subtle pressures of habit, Fromm's "anonymous authority," "common sense," and so on, to more obvious forms of overt coercion. [5]

We will call those statements made about the observed *by more than one person* capable of making the observations statements of *description*. By these standards, then, statement number one, if made about a dog we have observed barking, is a statement of description.

Statements of Inference

Suppose we have that dog before us and one of us says, "The dog is healthy." We have something to observe (the dog doing something), but can we observe the "health" in the way that we could observe the "barking"? The adjective "healthy" is usually applied to some internal condition that cannot be observed. We often qualify the word in a sentence, when it applies to us especially, with "I think I am" or "I feel" because we cannot observe all of the internal conditions that make up the description "healthy," in a way that a doctor might. (When we visit the doctor or take our dog to the veterinarian we are seeking to test our inference.)

Now you can imagine various observable actions that might indicate that the dog is healthy, but because you cannot observe the internal condition that is the ordinary-language meaning of "healthy," you cannot call this sentence a statement of description. As with the first sentence when made without having observed the dog, we are making a guess about the unknown on the basis of the known. Such statements we will call *statements of inference*.

---

[5] For those who feel that agreement alone is proof of anything, remedial reading in Hans Christian Andersen's "The Emperor's New Clothes" is recommended.

Statements of inference may be ranked according to their ability to be verified after they have been made. The range of verification runs from *immediately verifiable* to *unverifiable*. If you telephone a friend and make the inference, "My friend should be home at this hour, and therefore I infer that he will answer the telephone," you may determine whether your inference was correct within a matter of seconds. If, however, your phone rings and when you pick it up there is nobody on the other end of the line, you may make the inference that "I think a prankster called me" and never be able to verify who telephoned you or why.

Statements of inference may also be ranked according to their probability. Some guesses about the unknown are better guesses than others because some are based on more information or experience than others. Professional gamblers, insurance companies, and investors in the stock market are among those who "play the odds" by making the best inferences they can.

Statements of description are certain at the time of the observation; statements of inference are probable and possibly verifiable at a later time.

Many writers prefer to distinguish among the variety of sentences that will pass for our category of "inferential statements." A hypothesis that explains *why* something happened, and a guess about something that *will* happen might be separated. That is, a statement that explains a principle of why something happens in general (such as a law in physics), and a statement of prediction of a particular event made on the basis of that law might be distinguished. For most conversation, I do not believe that this distinction is essential. If I say that when I blow on this match flame the flame will go out, I am making a prediction about a future event on the basis of past events. My explanation may be inferentially based on certain laws of physics that are presumed to explain the phenomenon. Or, my explanation may be a descriptive generalization of past events—all of the other times I have blown on matches they have gone out. In either case, when we make a guess about the unknown on the basis of the known, we are in the realm of inference, whether the guess is a plausible explanation or a guess about a specific future event.

Probably most of human behavior operates on the basis of inference. This is true not only because any fool can spin out inferences but because most of the time we just do not have "the facts" on which to base our behavior. To make sense of what we do and to anticipate what we should do in the future, we must make assumptions. To recognize this does not mean that we may therefore abandon caution entirely. On the contrary, it means that we must be especially careful of these inferences, noting those that are more or less probable, recognizing the base of fact-description that supports the inferences, and be willing to alter our guesses when new information comes along.

Statements of Judgment

In the third statement in our list of four, "man's best friend" is not descriptive of anything that can be observed. It may be something of an inference based on what one man has felt (Barney's best friend *is* his dog), but others could make equally appropriate statements—"The dog is man's worst friend," for example. For statements of this kind, we bring into consideration our values. For one person a best friend is a dog; for another, a cat or canary; for another it might be his mother. Agreement proves little, because one is agreeing on values, not on observation. Such statements we will call statements of judgment. [6]

Chacun a son goût is the accepted judgment about judgments. You like your steaks well done, I like mine rare. You prefer the quarter system, I prefer the semester system. You are bored by this book, I think it's tremendous. *Chacun a son goût*.

The question of value, as Charles Morris has noted, cuts across all academic disciplines. Everybody has something to say about the nature of good or bad, and there is something to learn from every-

---

[6] You should note that we are using *judgment* in the sense of *value judgment*, and not in the sense in which the word is popularly used. In its common usage, *judgment* includes statements that we have called inferential—"I judge him to be over six feet tall"—in which case there is no preference stated about one's height.

bo[...] [...]eement among statements of judg-
m[...] [...] of description or inference. We
c[...] [...] an international congress of physi-
[...] [...] international congress of epicures or

[...] [...]dgments are often valuable because no
[...]ven expected. It is this range of prefer-
[...]at reveals and motivates the great variety
[...]ts cultural artifacts. If we were all of the
[...]ld all love the same person, desire the same
[...]same occupation. Although this is not the
[...] true that within a culture preferences do
[...]tandards of beauty, fashion, pleasure, and so
[...]e same way that one's language is learned. To
[...]gments are similar within a culture, judgments
[...] with descriptions. When everybody agrees
about some[...] t is easy for everybody to assume "it must be true."

We would do well to recognize judgments for what they are and
not expect or demand uniformity of judgment. What is important is
to realize when we are making judgments, to avoid stating judgments as if they were facts, and to be open to other choices. Such an
attitude not only improves the climate for communication and
understanding, it also may make each of us a more interesting
person.

Tautologies

The fourth statement about the dog is different still. We can observe
the four legs, we can observe the barking. But let us assume that the
sentence was not said in a way that meant that *this* dog has four legs
(count 'em) and is barking, but that *dog* is an animal that has four
legs and barks. When we are talking about *dog*, we are talking about
a word and how we wish to use it. We are giving a kind of definition
of *dog*, however useful that definition may be. In the same way, we
may say that "man is a featherless biped"; we are not saying that *this*
man seems to have no feathers and walks on two feet. We are saying

that we may define *man* (and *kangaroo*, for that matter) in terms of these characteristics. Such definitions of *dog* and *man* may be utterly useless; in any case, they are definitions and not statements of description.

Agreement about the meaning or use of words is the characteristic of a *tautology*. When one tests the accuracy of a statement not by checking it against an observed reality (description) or against an unobserved but probable event or explanation (inference) or against one's value system (judgment) but rather against a system of usage, one has a tautology. Thus, the previous sentence is also a tautology—for it tells how the author wishes to use these words. When, *by definition*, "a dog is . . ." or "justice is . . ." or "nonsense is . . ." the statement is a tautology and cannot be proved but only accepted or rejected within a system of usage.

It is possible, therefore, to classify the third sentence ("The dog is man's best friend") as a tautology, if by the sentence one seeks to define *dog* in terms of friendship. Probably this is the most common meaning of that sentence, anyway, since persons utter the sentence without reference to the nonverbal world of dogs biting children and mailmen.

Possibly because the verb *is* in English is required to do so much work and is used in so many senses, statements originally meant as statements of inference or judgment come to be used as tautologies. By sheer repetition of one man's preference for dogs the English-speaking world comes to define *dog* in terms of a value system.

Conversation becomes confused and communication breakdowns occur when different classifications of statements become confused. Under the pressure of an argument or because of linguistic ambiguities one may start with one meaning of a sentence and retreat to another. What often happens is that a speaker begins with an assertion that seems like a description but is extended so far as to be a generalization. When this speaker is challenged he changes his description into a tautology in order to rule out any exception. For example, one person may assert that "women are emotional and never calm in the face of a crisis." Another person replies that he knows a woman who is less emotional and more relaxed in a crisis than most men. To which the first speaker replies, "Well, that person isn't *really* a woman." He has, in effect, switched from talking about women to talking about his definition of women. This very argument, of course, frequently appeared in a variety of forms by critics of the Women's Liberation movement, with many of the "spokespeople" for the movement being reclassified by their critics as something other than women.

One final distinction is important. When one says of a chess game, "the bishop moves diagonally on his own color as far as the player wishes or until stopped by another chesspiece," the person may be indicating a tautology or may be stating a description of what he has seen in a chess game. What is important to determine here is the circumstances that prompted the statement. Two possibilities are suggested. Was the statement made on the basis of observation or on the basis of reading a book on chess? If the first is the case, then the statement is a description, and as a description it has no validity beyond that description. That is, under such circumstances the speaker can only state inferences about how the bishop will move in the future, for he must make a guess about the unknown on the basis of the known. If the second is the case, the speaker needs no observation in order to talk about the past, present or the future, for he has *defined* the bishop in terms of its moves. Any piece that does not move in accordance with this definition is not a bishop. Under the latter conditions the statement is a tautology.

Standards and Contexts

It is risky at best to attempt to classify any given statement as a description, inference, judgment, or tautology unless one knows the context in which it appears. (Fortunately, statements rarely appear in isolation—except, perhaps, on some teachers' examination questions.) We will say more about some aspects of context in the next chapter, but for now we should note the general problem of evaluating statements in isolation.

At the very least, there is the verbal context, the other sentences in which a statement for evaluation is embedded; this is what people usually seem to have in mind when they object to being quoted "out of context." More than that, however, there are the paralinguistic markers (mentioned in the next chapter) that make the exclamation "good luck!" a cheerful wish when said one way and the same words said in a different tone of voice mean "hah! you'll never succeed!" With written words out of verbal context it is impossible to know if the intention is one of encouragement or sarcasm. Then there is the context of time. What is an inference at one time may, at another time, be a statement of description. Most persons would probably like to classify the statement, "The earth is round" (or "The earth is a spheroid") as a statement of fact-description, and yet the measures that would enable that statement to meet the appropriate standards are quite recent. The social and cultural context should be considered, too. There are probably different intentions when a theologian or a geographer observes that in every life a little rain must fall.

Apart from such broad contexts, we must also consider the specific conditions under which any statement is made, for these will have to be tested against our standards in order to evaluate the statement. The statement "It is raining," for example, is a statement of description only if one has had that experience we call "observing the weather." If the statement is made only on the basis of hearing what sounds like thunder and a noise that sounds like water plopping on the roof, the sentence is an inference based on these experiences. The more precise speaker would say "I hear what sounds like thunder and what sounds like water on the roof, and so I infer that it is raining." If this sounds picayune it may be because it would seem that usually no harm would come from guessing it was raining when it was not. But in most of our lives we must *act on inferences*, not on descriptions. At such times knowing we are making inferences might make us more cautious. To say "the right turn signal on the car in front of me is blinking [description] and so I infer that he will turn [inference]" should make us more cautious about acting than if we say "the car in front of me is going to turn" as if our inference had the accuracy of a description.

One way to develop a keener critical attitude toward evaluating statements is to imagine a variety of contexts and specific conditions which might have provoked any one statement. Although in one sense this is working backward, using our imagination on sample statements can prepare us to be more critical of our own speaking habits and those of others. Consider the following examples and for each try to imagine different contexts, different conditions under which each statement might be made, resulting in different evaluations (and classifications) for each.

1. Nice guys finish last.
2. All roads lead to Rome.
3. February is the coldest month.
4. Coke is the pause that refreshes.
5. Lincoln: a great man, a great car!

Variations on the Theme

There are useful variations on the four kinds of sentences we have been discussing. Because the titles are descriptive, little explanation will be given.

Personal descriptions (or to-me facts): "I have a toothache" or "I am sleepy." Here, verification by more than one observer is difficult or impossible.

Reports of descriptions: "The capital of Tibet is Lhasa"; "George Washington was born in 1732." The tests of descriptions have been met by qualified observers, but the person making the statement may not have been able to make the tests.

Reports of inferences: "There is no life on the planet Mars"; "Lee Harvey Oswald was mentally deranged"; "Patrick Henry said 'Give me liberty or give me death.'" The first statement is, at this date, only an inference based on the best evidence; in the future, such a statement may be proven or disproven. The second statement poses several problems, including the inference that Oswald shot President Kennedy ("legal proof" by the Warren Commission puts the guilt of Oswald "beyond a reasonable doubt," though such proof has not been accepted universally). Another difficulty with the sentence is the meaning of "mentally deranged." For some, any person who shoots another is "mentally deranged"—this being one possible definition for mental derangement. If one takes other definitions, this condition can only be inferential. The third sentence is popularly thought to be a report of a description. But a little investigation will show that our record of the speech is one that first appeared in Henry's biography written twenty years later. One may infer that the famous phrase was composed not by Henry but by his biographer.

These four choices appear to extend along a linear continuum, with one pole represented by statements of description and the other extreme representing tautologies. We might then place inferences next to statements of description, and put statements of judgment between the inferences and the tautologies. The polar extremes would at least remind us of the contrast between sense-data orientations (for descriptions) and system-orientations which characterize tautologies. And there is some convenience to thinking of inferences as closer to descriptions than to tautologies, and to thinking that our judgments are probably closer to our individual or social criteria (systems) of good or bad, ugly or beautiful, and so on, than to the sense data.

Perhaps a better diagram, however, would be circular:

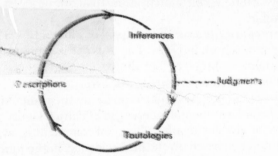

The circular model might at least serve to remind us that even our statements of description are based on and expressed in words or other symbols, and that these, in turn, are meaningful only as a part of some system. If to this we add arrows suggesting a developmental process they might be such as are expressed in the circular diagram: descriptions leading to inferences in anticipation of the rules of person isn't *really* a woman." He has, in effect, switched from talking about women to talking about his definition of women. This very argument, of course, frequently appeared in a variety of forms by critics of the Women's Liberation movement, with many of the "spokespeople" for the movement being reclassified by their critics as something other than women.

One final distinction is important. When one says of a chess game, "the bishop moves diagonally on his own color as far as the player wishes or until stopped by another chesspiece," the person may be indicating a tautology or may be stating a description of what he has seen in a chess game. What is important to determine here is the circumstances that prompted the statement. Two possibilities are suggested. Was the statement made on the basis of observation or on the basis of reading a book on chess? If the first is the case, then the statement is a description, and as a description it has no validity beyond that description. That is, under such circumstances the speaker can only state inferences about how the bishop will move in the future, for he must make a guess about the unknown on the basis of the known. If the second is the case, the speaker needs no observation in order to talk about the past, present or the future, for he has *defined* the bishop in terms of its moves. Any piece that does not move in accordance with this definition is not a bishop. Under the latter conditions the statement is a tautology.

Standards and Contexts

It is risky at best to attempt to classify any given statement as a description, inference, judgment, or tautology unless one knows the context in which it appears. (Fortunately, statements rarely appear in isolation—except, perhaps, on some teachers' examination questions.) We will say more about some aspects of context in the next chapter, but for now we should note the general problem of evaluating statements in isolation.

At the very least, there is the verbal context, the other sentences in which a statement for evaluation is embedded; this is what people usually seem to have in mind when they object to being quoted "out of context." More than that, however, there are the paralinguistic markers (mentioned in the next chapter) that make the exclamation "good luck!" a cheerful wish when said one way and the same words said in a different tone of voice mean "hah! you'll never succeed!" With written words out of verbal context it is impossible to know if the intention is one of encouragement or sarcasm. Then there is the context of time. What is an inference at one time may, at another time, be a statement of description. Most persons would probably like to classify the statement, "The earth is round" (or "The earth is a spheroid") as a statement of fact-description, and yet the measures that would enable that statement to meet the appropriate standards are quite recent. The social and cultural context should be considered, too. There are probably different intentions when a theologian or a geographer observes that in every life a little rain must fall.

Apart from such broad contexts, we must also consider the specific conditions under which any statement is made, for these will have to be tested against our standards in order to evaluate the statement. The statement "It is raining," for example, is a statement of description only if one has had that experience we call "observing the weather." If the statement is made only on the basis of hearing what sounds like thunder and a noise that sounds like water plopping on the roof, the sentence is an inference based on these experiences. The more precise speaker would say "I hear what sounds like thunder and what sounds like water on the roof, and so I infer that it is raining." If this sounds picayune it may be because it would seem that usually no harm would come from guessing it was raining when it was not. But in most of our lives we must *act on inferences*, not on descriptions. At such times knowing we are making inferences might make us more cautious. To say "the right turn signal on the car in front of me is blinking [description] and so I infer that he will turn [inference]" should make us more cautious about acting than if we say "the car in front of me is going to turn" as if our inference had the accuracy of a description.

One way to develop a keener critical attitude toward evaluating statements is to imagine a variety of contexts and specific conditions which might have provoked any one statement. Although in one concept especially useful, for when one performs a specific operation he is moving from the verbal to the nonverbal level. An operational definition is the instruction for performing some task, the observation of which will explain the concept. If one wants to know what the color "red" is, he may be told to do any of several things in which "red" will appear—"cut your finger and the color of the blood that comes out will be red." Less painful would be the instructions to go to a stoplight and see the color of the light when all of the cars are in line waiting. There are many other possibilities, of course.

Social scientists may operationally define a specific stimulus in an experiment as "anything that causes the rat to jump the grid." Professors may operationally define a "superior student" as anybody who scores over 95 per cent correct on a given test. A librarian may operationally define as a "disturbance" anything that makes more than 5 per cent of the readers complain that they are unable to read efficiently. In such cases, there is no point in arguing about what a "stimulus" *really* is, or a "superior student" *really* is, or a "disturbance" *really* is. The concept of operationalism assumes the utility of saying "for our purposes." And if one operational definition does not suit the purposes of another individual, he is free to select another operation. Whatever the choice, such an attitude about language has the advantage of agreement through observation.

There is a limitation in the concept of operationalism. If we require all of our statements to be operational before we can trust them or regard them as useful, the value of speculative systems is lost. Often a theory is proposed long before there are ways of making it operational. Indeed, it is the very construction of the theoretical system that opens the ways for new kinds of operations. F. S. C. Northrop[8] has stressed this:

> Again and again in the history of science deductively formulated theories such as Albert Einstein's theory of the finite universe have been constructed as answers to theoretical questions, and at the time of their construction no conceivable operation for testing them was at hand.

[8] F. S. C. Northrop, *The Logic of the Sciences and Humanities* (New York: World Publishing Co., 1959, by arrangement with Macmillan), p. 130.

some system, and tautologies which are revised to correspond to new descriptions and new inferences. If such a model is at all useful, we must think of the circular process as continuous and not a single movement around the circle. In our diagram we might also want to leave the category of judgments just outside of the circular path which we have described; clearly not all statements of judgment pertain to the mutual dependence and revision of description, inference making, and tautologies.

The scientific method does not deal with statements of judgment as we have presented them. But the other three kinds of statements are the basis of the scientific method. Descriptions of sense data will change, depending on the system in use at the time. What was described by the best science of two hundred years ago in terms of *heat* is now described in terms of *thermodynamics*. Systems will change on the basis of new sense data recorded.[7] The matter of "race" has changed in this century from descriptions of biological data to descriptions of social behavior. The scientific method, the attempt to organize the most scrutinized experiences, is a continuous process. How we personally organize our own experiences *could* be almost as careful, but my personal inferences about how people behave, on the basis of my own descriptions of my experiences, does not permit me to make the judgment that man is usually so very conscientious.

An Operational Attitude

The concept of *operationalism*, developed both by John Dewey and, especially, by the physicist P. W. Bridgman, has made it possible to restrict and test many sentences that previously would have been considered unverifiable. Semanticists have found the

---

[7] Actually, even within the scientific community, systems do not change *solely* on the basis of new sense data recorded. Max Planck has remarked, "A new scientific truth does not triumph by convincing its opponents and making them see the light, but rather because its opponents eventually die, and a new generation grows up that is familiar with it." (Quoted in Max Planck, *Scientific Autobiography and Other Papers* (New York: Gaynor, 1949, 33).

With further theoretical investigation it often turns out to be possible to derive theorems which do permit the theory to be put to an experimental test. Were all concepts in a scientific theory solely operationally defined concepts, it would be difficult to understand how this could be the case. Then there could be no scientific theory without the operation for verifying it automatically being present.

Operational definitions can improve many conversations by making more specific some of the loose terms in any kind of sentence and by rendering verifiable statements that would otherwise be unverifiable. But where the subject is admittedly speculative, and valuable for that very reason, the criterion of being operational must not be demanded.

Summary

The study of language leads us to an apparent dilemma. On the one hand, we seem to have the freedom to describe the world in many ways; and yet on the other hand, no matter how we describe the world we will be distorting it through our words. We have *abstracted from* and *projected to* that which we wish to describe. *Whatever* we say a thing *is*, it is *not that*.

If you have never thought about this problem before, the realization may be demoralizing. Some students are so shocked that they think they should totally accept nihilism or become mystics or Trappist monks. If one can never speak "truth," one does better to not speak at all. This is one alternative.

But this wears off. (Usually.) Talking is necessary. Often it is fun. And besides, the counterargument goes, we seem to do all right within those limitations. This puts us back to where we started, but with one important difference. Now we are aware of the restrictions and inadequacies of our language, and being thus aware, we will try to be more careful in our speaking and thinking. Some standards within the limitations of language must be established if we are to organize our experiences into meaningful utterances.

In this chapter, we have examined a framework for comparing

different kinds of symbolic expressions, a framework limited at one end by statements of immediate sense data, and at the other by statements about some verbal system. Because our language does not directly indicate these different kinds of statements through special symbols, it is important that we be personally critical. Such an awareness may prevent much needless confusion that results from arguing about the use of a word as part of a system as if one were arguing about some verifiable description of sense data.

Statements that report sense data are called *statements of description*, and those that report definitions, rules for usage, and constructs within a system are called *tautologies*. Within these bounds lie *inferential statements*, which rely on both observation and system, and which state a guess about the unknown on the basis of the known. Value judgments, a fourth kind of statement, are determined within a personal or cultural system of values. Most sentences cannot be easily classified as just one of these four types unless the conditions that have prompted the statement are also known.

With the application of the operational principle, statements can be related to observable sense data. At these lower levels of abstraction, the chances for understanding and agreement among different persons are greatly increased.

SIX

WHEN PEOPLE
TALK WITH PEOPLE

Years ago, a popular phonograph record produced by Stan
Freberg presented a short conversation between two persons,
Marsha and John. The conversation began like this:
    "John—"
    "Marsha . . ."
    "John . . ."
    "Marsha . . ."
    "John . . ."
    "Marsha . . ."
    (Using the above dialogue as a basis, the clever reader can
extrapolate the entire three-minute conversation.)
    The printed form does not convey what the recording
artists did with only two words. They were able to indicate
differences in meaning by speaking the words with varied
inflections and in different tones of voice. In fact, so skillful
was the performance that several radio stations banned the
harmless record from the air as "too suggestive."
    The vocal variations on a theme of two words illustrate two
simple but very important points about communication: (1) that
the spoken word can have many different intended and
interpreted meanings depending upon *how* it is said; and (2) that

a phrase or even a single word can serve many functions depending upon its context and the way in which it is expressed. The sensitive conversant, the diplomat, the therapist are well aware of the many purposes of communication that any word or phrase may serve, and yet this awareness is frequently ignored when persons give too much attention to conventional semantics of word–thing relationships. Without such an awareness we must either disregard much, perhaps most, of everyday conversation, or we are likely to totally misinterpret the conversational meaning of all that talk.

Paralanguage and Metacommunication

In everyday communication there are always more than words that pass between persons. There are also cues that indicate to the persons how the spoken words are to be interpreted. One writer [1] has suggested we interpret all verbal messages on two levels: the *report*, what might be considered the "literal meaning" of the words, and the *command*, which is the apparent purpose or intention or function of those words. Thus the John–Marsha dialogue on paper appears to be a repetition of reports, but because of the varying inflection, loudness, and tone of voice, as well as the spoken words preceding and following each "John" or "Marsha," we seem to have a great number of different commands.

Leo Rosten in his delightful book, *The Joys of Yiddish* [2] presents a treasury of similar examples, suggesting that part of the richness of Yiddish lies in the many meanings of some words as determined by a "Yiddish tone of voice." He tells the story of a Russian man who received a telegram from his wife which read: DOCTOR SAYS OPERATE OPERATE. The husband then cabled back immediately this telegram: DOCTOR SAYS OPERATE OPERATE. This exchange aroused the suspicions of the authorities who immediately investigated to see if this was some secret code. But the husband protested that the authorities were misreading the tele-

---

[1] Paul Watzlawick, et al., *The Pragmatics of Human Communication*. New York: W. W. Norton, 1967, Ch. 2.

[2] Leo Rosten, *The Joys of Yiddish* (London: Penguin Books, 1968).

gram; clearly what they said was: "Doctor says operate. *Operate?*" And the reply: "Doctor says operate, *operate!*"

The general name given to meaningful differences in tone of voice, inflection, rate, pitch, volume, and so forth is *paralanguage*. In ordinary face-to-face conversation, however, even paralanguage describes only a part of all that is communicated to give particular interpretations (or to suggest particular intentions) to any given expression. The social setting (a cocktail party or a funeral), the vast array of nonverbal cues (facial expression, hair style, clothing, eye behavior, posture, distance between the people conversing, and gestures), and even the difference between what we expect to hear and what we think we hear all render apparently similar reports into apparently different commands. Some writers have called all such aspects of communication *metacommunication*. (We should note that metacommunication is sometimes used with quite different meanings, including the technical language used for analyzing communication.)

As mentioned earlier, most of traditional semantic studies and even a large portion of general semantics literature have so stressed the word–thing relationship (the semantic dimension in Morris's three-part scheme) and have relied so much on printed or written words that paralinguistic and functional considerations of meaning have been overlooked. But unless we pay attention to these concerns we will run into the same kind of problem that foreign language students face when they are too literal minded about the language they are studying, reporting one's state of health when asked "How are you?" or, in Japan, giving an honest answer to the question, "Where are you going?" Viewed one way, the two questions seem completely different; viewed *functionally*, the two "questions" mean about the same thing: "Hello."

Phatic Communion

Small talk, uninspired greetings, and idle chatter are among the description of a fundamental type of communication that Bronislaw Malinowski called *phatic communion*. To show that we welcome communication, that we are friendly, or that we at least acknowledge the presence of another person, we exchange words. In English we do not have special words for this function of communication, though phatic communion tends to be rather unimaginative. We say, "How are You?" or "Hello," or "Nice day." There may be variations based on geography ("Howdy!") or familiarity ("Hi ya, Baby!") or specific conditions ("Cold enough for ya?"). Whatever the words, the speaker is saying, in effect, "I see you and I am friendly." The channels of communication are opened.

In phatic communion, the specific words exchanged are not important. This is illustrated in the story of a U.S. businessman who, while traveling to Europe for the first time, finds himself seated across from a Frenchman at lunch. Neither speaks the other's language, but each smiles a greeting. As the wine is served, the Frenchman raises his glass and gesturing to the American says, "*Bon appétit!*" The American does not understand and replies, "Ginzberg." No other words are exchanged at lunch. That evening at dinner, the two again sit at the same table and again the Frenchman greets the American with the wine, saying, "*Bon appétit!*" to which the American replies "Ginzberg." The waiter notices this peculiar exchange and, after dinner, calls the American aside to explain that "the Frenchman is not giving his name—he is wishing you a good appetite; he is saying that he hopes you enjoy your meal." The following day the American seeks out the Frenchman at lunch, wishing to correct his error. At the first opportunity the American raises his glass and says, "*Bon appétit!*" To which the Frenchman proudly replies, "Ginzberg."

Although in this story the ignorance of a common language made more significant communication impossible, it was the exchange of simple words like *Bon appétit* (and *Ginzberg*) that broke the tension of silence and expressed friendship. Without the small talk first there can be no "big talk" later.

The only rule that seems to apply to phatic communion is that the "subject" of the communication be such that each party can say something about it. That is why everybody talks about the weather. The important thing is to talk—and this is why so much of phatic communion begins with a question, for a question requires a reply.

We do not request specific information in phatic communion

and we are not expected to reply with precision or accuracy. If we are greeted with a "How are you?" we do not reply as we might if our doctor asked the question. When we are precise the result is likely to be humorous, as when James Thurber was once asked, "How's your wife?" and replied, "Compared to *what?*"

Specific information is sought in one kind of greeting, however. Members of secret organizations sometimes speak in code when they meet to determine whether each knows the password, special handshake, or other symbol. If the answer to the secret question is not precise, then the other is not regarded as a brother Mason or sister Theta or whatever, and subsequent communication will be prevented. Such coded phatic communion dates from times when members of such organizations might be persecuted if discovered. Among some "secret organizations" today, the reverse seems to be true. The coded greeting is often expressed loudly, more for the benefit of the outsiders than for the "secret" members. Phatic communion is usually the most casual, even careless, form of communication. The stories of persons passing through receiving lines and saying something like "I just killed my mother-in-law," which is met with a smile and a "Fine, I hope you're enjoying yourself" are well known. They illustrate what little significance is attached to phatic communion, so little that the speaker is not even listened to. In such extreme cases, however, we may wonder to what extent the channels of communication have been opened after that exchange of noises. In any case, it seems that we prefer some noise to no noise.

Blocking of Communication

A second function of communication is the opposite of the first. Just as we rarely open a conversation with "I see you and I am friendly," when this may be the real "message" of our greeting, we rarely prevent further communication by saying directly, "I don't want to talk to you anymore." This is said sometimes, to be sure. But there are more sophisticated ways that we have mastered.

There are the dismissal reactions "Ha!" "That's crazy!" "Yeah,

I'll bet!" and so forth. Whether the speaker intends these to block communication or whether they merely function in this way is often difficult to determine. In either case it takes but a few well chosen reactions to end a conversation—and a few more to end a friendship.

Then there are the guarded utterances or verbal grunts that seem to show a lack of interest in speaker or subject: "Oh, really?" "I see—," "Indeed," or "Hmm."

These brief snips of uninterested responses will end a conversation, and often large hunks of verbiage will achieve the same end. Either the language seems to say nothing or it is so difficult to decipher that it does not seem worth the effort. A favorite technique of naughty children, students taking examinations, and some U.S. Senators is to talk on and on about anything irrelevant to the subject at hand.

Recording–Transmitting Functions

One definition of teaching goes something like this: "Teaching is the transmission of the professor's notes into the students' notebooks without their having passed through the minds of either." A few years ago it was reported that a professor at a large midwestern college put his lectures on tape and had the tape recorder sent into his classroom and played every day. Weeks later, when he stopped into the room to see if all was going well, he found, on each student's desk, another machine recording the lectures. Allowing for the hyperboles here, these stories illustrate a basic function of communication, where the individual performs like a precise and self-contained transmitting and recording machine.

In one sense, all communication is a process of transmitting some information that is received by another. This is one definition of communication. But as we note the variety of ways in which we can describe the kind and purpose of a message sent, the category of transmitting-recording seems insufficient. The category is useful only for the most neutral exchanges of information, messages without intent to be instrumental, compliment the listener, let off steam, and so on. Thus, asking when the next bus leaves and being told;

asking what time it is, and being told; reporting or hearing the news, weather, classroom lectures, and so on, all might be examples of this function of communication.

Instrumental Communication

When we say something and something happens as the result of our speaking, then our comments have been instrumental in causing that event to happen. The instrumental function of communication is one of its most common purposes. We request a secretary to type three copies of a letter. We ask a friend at dinner to pass the butter. We order a salesman out of the house.

The category of instrumental communication is loose enough to allow for several kinds of statements. There are statements that are clearly instrumental in their wording, for which the result correlates with the language. If we say "Shut the door" and the door is then shut, we may assume that the noise we made was influential in the shutting of the door. There are also statements for which the results cannot be so easily attributed to our utterances. If on a day planned for a picnic it is raining and so we sing, "Rain, rain go away"—and the rain does stop—it would be immodest to assume that our words caused that action. Much of prayer has been traditionally instrumental, and if the faithful believe that some prayers "have been answered," we could say that for these people the prayer was an instrumental communication. We will touch on this subject again when we discuss ritual and the magic function of communication.

Some statements are instrumental in intent or effect, but are not phrased as such. For example, if you want the salt passed to you, you may request it directly (instrumental) or you might comment that the food needs salt (transmitting information). If a wife wants a new fur coat, she may request it directly or she may comment on how well dressed her husband seems, especially when compared to her (apparently an effective technique). One instrumental request may result in a different instrumental action, as when commercial airlines do not ask passengers to stop smoking but to "observe the no smoking sign."

One characteristic of some instrumental statements is a faint resemblance between manner of speaking and the requested action itself. One sometimes speaks as if his words *were* instruments, as a belaying pin or rawhide whip are instruments. The voice (see metacommunication) does its best to imitate the desired action, as do voices instrumentally cheering at a football game, "Push 'em back, push 'em back, w-a-a-a-a-y back!"

Affective Communication

Communication in which the message is the emotional feelings of the speaker toward a listener is known as *affective communication*. Compliments, praise and flattery, and also snide and cutting remarks may be so classified.

There are affective elements in many of the functions of communication. Phatic communion may contain praise, as when old friends greet by saying, "You're looking great!" As noted in the previous section, instrumental purposes are often best served through affective communication, too.

It seems to be part of the woman's role in our society to use more affective communication than does the opposite sex. Where tradition has not given women authority in all situations, women have had to achieve their goals indirectly. And this indirection may be reflected in instrumental desires disguised in affective language. The wife who says to her husband, "You look so handsome all dressed up," might be requesting a new wardrobe for herself or be asking to go out to dinner, rather than just complimenting her husband.

The nonaffective language of fact and description or the language of clear and explicit requests need not be any more desirable than it is common in interpersonal communications. We admire and respect the clarity of the scientist in writing his report, but we may find him less explicit during his courtship. Perhaps the reason is that whereas the scientist communicates to himself and to others pursuing one goal, the diplomats or the lovers may not be sure they are pursuing the same goal.

A study of the social gestures of dating, which I once made in an attempt to discover what was "meant" when a man held the door for his date or failed to open the door, and so on, certainly indicated this. Each sex had its own mythology for the purpose of the gesture. To the woman, the man performed the task out of respect for Woman. To the man, he performed the task because he "had to" if he was going to get anywhere. Again, the man's purpose even in the nonverbal language was far more instrumental than the woman's. If the words and actions were more specific, it would not be possible for the sexes to maintain their mutual self-delusion.

Affective language is also *convincing* language. In many cases a person would not do something if asked to do it directly; he would be too aware of reasons that he might not be able to accept. We seem to prefer to do things we think we want to do, not things we are told to do. There is a story of an experiment performed by a university class on its professor. The class set out as a group to apply simple learning theory (reward-punishment) on the professor in order to force him to do something he would not ordinarily do and certainly not do if requested. The emotional rewards and "punishments," though nonverbal in this case, are comparable to the use of affective language for instrumental purposes. The class decided it would try to move the professor into a corner from which he would deliver his lectures. The reinforcement was of the kind professors like best, interested expressions on student faces, passionate note taking at his every word, smiles at his whimsy and laughter at his wit. These responses, when appropriate, were made whenever the professor moved in the direction of the desired corner. When he moved in the other direction the class responded with looks of boredom, gazing out the windows, shuffling of feet, and the other academic behaviors one has rehearsed since childhood. As the story goes, by the end of the semester the professor was, indeed, giving his lectures from the corner of the room.

Although this story may be apocryphal, affective communication in a variety of situations does "move" the listener in a way that direct requests would not. The salesman knows it (I'll make a special deal just for you"), the professor knows it (I'm sure that your studies of Artaud and Beckett have led you to ask . . ."), the lover knows it. Most persons recognize the influence of words on the ego. (I'm sure that *you*, dear reader, are very sensitive to the communication process. . . .) To make another person feel good (or bad) through language is a rather common and vital function of communication.

It is possible to characterize attitudes of speakers toward their listeners on the basis of instrumental-affective content. One unpublished study[3] of Mexican attitudes toward male and female members of the Holy Family discovered that the language used toward male statues in a church was almost entirely instrumental in content, whereas the language used before the statue of the Virgin was highly affective. This distinction mirrored the differences in language used by children toward their parents in the average Mexican home. It is possible that degrees of anger, hostility, authority, and so on, can be measured by the comparitive content of instrumental and affective language in our everyday expressions.

Many criticisms of the U.S. visitor or resident abroad have their basis in a lack of affective communication and a preponderance of instrumental communication. As a pragmatic people, we may have a cultural tendency to "get down to business," to be impersonal. Former Secretary of State John Foster Dulles is often quoted in Latin America as having said with some pride that "the U.S. does not have friends; it has interests." If others are treated as "interests" when they are more accustomed to being treated as "brothers" or at least "cousins," surely they will resent the change. The nonaffective communication may be honest, fair, sincere. But to one who does not expect it, the communication is cold, unfeeling, mechanical.

"Better understanding through communication" is a popular slogan. Too often what is meant is an improvement in semantics, an increase in the clarity of what we *mean*. We must not forget the affective aspects of communication, and must strive for an increase in the interpersonal attraction that we *feel*.

Catharsis

When you are angry or disturbed or hurt, physically or mentally, probably you give expression to your feelings. It is curious that

[3] Cynthia Nelson, "Saints and Sinners: Parallels in the Sex-Role Differentiation in the Family of Saints and in the Family of Man in a Mexican Peasant Village" (mimeographed, N.D.).

expressions, which could be as personal as the feelings that evoke them, are rather stylized and predictable within a language. Words like *ouch!* or *oh!* are spoken by a people who speak English, whereas our neighbors who speak Spanish will say *ay!* when they express a comparable feeling. Grunts may be the only universal expression of catharsis.

When pain or frustration is sufficient, our cathartic expression becomes more obviously symbolic. We move from the "ouch!" to words that might be used in other ways, most often words that are socially disapproved of. We swear or curse or substitute words that sound something like the popular curses we long ago learned were "adult" and special. We find that different kinds of expressions for releasing tension are appropriate among different ages and occupations. A sailor who is angry is not expected to say "Oh, goodness me!" and an angry nun is not expected to sound like a sailor.

It is a safe cultural generalization that in most societies of the world, the sex roles and expectations are clearly, symbolically, distinguished between males and females. They dress differently, play different games as children, walk differently, and are expected to assume different social roles. They are also expected to talk differently. In the United States and in a few other parts of the world, however, sex differences have tended to be diminished. The late 1960s saw a rise in unisex fashions in clothing as well as the passing of many laws designed to break this distinction (labeled "discrimination") in employment, membership in organizations, and so on. It also was a period when many words, particularly those most frequently associated with cathartic expressions (swearing, exclamations, and so on) went unisex. (It is significant that some women were free to swear like men, not the other way around.) It was often reported that during protest marches and speeches that characterized this period, policemen would become most upset by the taunts of women, particularly college-age women. The explanation was simply that most policemen come from backgrounds where the sex-role distinction, including language style, was still an important distinction, and therefore when girls used some choice "male" epithets to taunt the police they seemed to be threatening the whole social and moral order.

The physical stimulus finds expression in a symbol. This symbol eventually ceases to stand for, directly, anything in the outside world except an attitude toward whatever produced it. We move from physical sensation to verbal assault on that sensation ("damn it!") to mere release of tension.

The idea of cursing a situation dates to times when the belief in magic language was more common. There was a time when "God damn you" was meant as a magic curse to bring about suffering. The transference into such symbols was a step above the infantile reaction of actually attacking the offending person or object. Children may be observed to run into a wall and then physically retaliate against the wall, kicking it and saying "you mean old wall." But when the child's father runs into the wall and says "damn it!" (or, if the child is there, "darn it!") he probably is not talking to the wall. He is simply relieving his tension in symbols that have long evolved from their literal meaning.

Because expressions of catharsis have no referential meaning, any word may serve the cathartic function. Probably each person has some favorite expressions for releasing anger. If you were to prepare a list of cathartic expressions, ranking them according to the degree of tension to be released, you might find it an easy task, too, which indicates that there are personal favorites for a hierarchy of catharsis. The meaning of any of these expressions is to be found in what they do for us, not in a dictionary or in what they do for anybody else. Through repetition we give our select swear words added significance, so that with each new experience and repeated expression we may recall the release of tension from past experiences.

If you have studied another language, you may have learned the kinds of swear words that are most common in that language. In the literal translation they may not seem to "do much for you." Obviously, they cannot, for they have not yet come to be associated with the experiences that give them meaning. This same observation might be made for all words, but the language of catharsis, associated with the strongest of emotions, is the most extreme example of the general principle.

Magic[4]

The belief in the magic power of words exists in all cultures and takes the form of superstitions, instrumental curses, aspects of most religions, and minor forms of wishful thinking. At the root of the attitude of magic is the assumption that words are part of the thing to which they refer and, often, that words precede the "thing" (such as expressed in the Bible, "In the beginning was the Word"). Another quality of the magic attitude of words is that words "stand for things" in the sense that a friend "stands for" a bride or groom in a marriage by proxy. With this belief it follows that one can alter a thing by altering its word. If I write your name on a piece of paper and burn it, you, too, will burn, or at least suffer pain. Words, in the magical interpretation, must be treated with the same care as one would treat what the words stand for.

A common example of the belief in word-magic is the hesitancy to speak of possible dangers. If, on an airplane, you remark about the possibility of crashing, fellow passengers may turn on you as if your utterance of the possibility might just cause that to happen. In some cases, of course, it may be simply that others do not wish to think of unpleasant things; but the manner and intensity of the reply often indicates a very real fear of the words. If the belief in a magic function of cummunication seems immature (that is, not at all what *you* would think or do), ask yourself whether in a plane, you ever avoided such "thoughts" or whether you ever thought "we will not crash, we will not crash." For better or for worse, the belief that thinking or saying words will have some effect on what the words stand for is an example of the magic function of communication.

In many religions the magic function of language is still present. One would expect this of any institution that is centuries old and seeks to conserve the language and ritual of the past. The distinction

[4] Susanne Langer includes the magic function of language as part of "ritual." She writes, "Magic . . . is not a method, but a language; it is part and parcel of that greater phenomenon, ritual, which is the language of religion." (*Philosophy in a New Key* [Cambridge: Harvard University Press, 1942], p. 39.) Although this may have a historical basis, and although magic and ritual are also clearly related today, I find it useful to make a distinction between the two.

between transubstantiation and consubstantiation of the Roman Catholic and Protestant sects is, in part, the difference in attitude toward the magic function of language. Do the bread and wine *become* the body and blood of Christ, or do they merely symbolize the body and blood? There are other examples in religions. The Anglican and Roman Catholic faiths retain rituals for the exorcising of spirits from a haunted house. One may wish to make a distinction between these examples and examples of words that call for the intercession of a divine spirit (such as prayers of petition) where the effect is produced not by the utterance of the words but by the action upon the words by another being. The difference is the difference between Ali Baba saying "Open Sesame!" (and having the cave door open because of the magic in the words) and having the words heard by a god who then opens the door. In the latter case we have an example of instrumental communication.[5]

Symbols associated with persons have long been recognized for their magical associations. Personal names have been regarded as "part of the person," so that what is done to the name results in affecting the person. (Elements of this attitude are still very common today, as when parents give their child the name of somebody important to them so that the child will be like his namesake.) The magical attitude toward personal names requires that these names not be taken in vain or, in some cases, not even uttered.

> Here the name is never a mere symbol, but is part of the personal property of its bearer; property which is exclusively and jealously reserved to him. . . . Georg von der Gabelentz, in his book on the science of language, mentions the edict of a Chinese emperor of the third century B.C. whereby a pronoun in the first person, that had been legitimately in popular use, was henceforth reserved to him along. . . . It is said of the Eskimos that for them man consists of three elements —body, soul, and name. And in Egypt, too, we find a similar conception, for there the physical body of man was thought to be accompanied, on the one hand by his Ka, or double, and on the other, by his name, as a sort of spiritual double. . . . Under Roman law a slave had no legal name, because he could not function as a legal person.[6]

[5] Some students are unimpressed by the distinction.
[6] Ernst Cassirer, *Language and Myth* (New York: Dover Publications, N.D.), pp. 50–51.

Cassirer points out, too, that this attitude toward personal names was held by the early Christians, and hence today Christians still say "In Jesus' name" instead of "In Christ."

The belief in the magic function of language is based on assumptions that are quite opposed to the discipline of semantics, which regards words as conventional and convenient and without necessary associations with persons or objects in themselves. There is a sense, however, in which words do have "power." Words have the "power" to limit our thought, for example, though this is a different sense of the word "power." With rumor, with labels that evoke signal reactions, and with labels we try to live up to, we see some effects of the "power" of words. Such powers, however, are not magical, for they are not to be found *in* the words. Rather, the powers are social, and thus they are effective only to the degree that we accept our language without evaluation and respond to words without evaluation. When we understand and evaluate our language habits this social magic spell of words is broken.

Ritual

The scene is a Senate Subcommittee hearingroom on October 1, 1963. A sixty-year-old convicted murderer, Joseph M. Valachi, calmly reports to the investigators some of the history and methods of the crime organization known as Cosa Nostra. According to the press reports, the witness appeared comfortable throughout his testimony until he described his induction into the organization. Emanuel Perlmutter[7] of the *New York Times* reports:

> Valachi said he had been taken into a large room, where 30 or 35 men were sitting at a long table.
>
> "There was a gun and a knife on the table," Valachi testified. "I sat at the edge. They sat me down next to Maranzaro. I repeated some words in Sicilian after him." . . .
>
> "You live by the gun and knife, and die by the gun and knife." . . .

[7] Emanuel Perlmutter, "Valachi Names 5 as Crime Chiefs in New York Area," *New York Times*, October 2, 1963, p. 28.

The witness said Maranzaro had then given him a piece of paper that was set afire in his hand.

"I repeated in Sicilian, 'This is the way I burn if I betray the organization.'" . . .

Valachi said the men at the table then "threw out a number," with each man holding up any number of fingers from one to five. The total was taken. Starting with Maranzaro, the sum was then counted off around the table. The man on whom the final number fell was designated as Valachi's "godfather" in the family. Valachi said the lot had fallen to Bonanno.

The witness said that he had then had his finger pricked by a needle held by Bonanno to show he was united to Bonanno by blood. Afterward, Valachi continued, all those present joined hands in a bond to the organization.

Valachi said he was given two rules in Cosa Nostra that night—one concerning allegiance to it and another a promise not to possess another member's wife, sister or daughter.

For the first time, the witness grew grim. "This is the worst thing I can do, to tell about the ceremony," he said. "This is my doom, telling it to you and the press."

If the ceremony Valachi described seems strange to us, stranger still is the fear of his "doom" caused by revealing that secret. For a tough-minded criminal who reported that for him "killing was like breathing," who gave evidence about the methods and men of the Cosa Nostra, why should the most fearful disclosure be his report of some remote and grisly rite performed years ago? The answer to that question is part of the answer to why some rituals affect almost all of us.

Few organizations or institutions have rituals quite like the Cosa Nostra. The language of the rituals of secret organizations, social fraternities, lodges, and some religious or political organizations is kept secret, known only to their members. But the language of other rituals—patriotic, religious, academic, and so on—is not kept private. Nevertheless, an oath of allegiance or a communal prayer can affect the nervous system as no statement of fact or judgment can.

Ritual is sometimes described as the behavioral part of a mythology. The mythology may be for almost any purpose, but consistently it emphasizes a sense of community among its members and a sense of permanence. To participate in a ritual is to participate in a community, often one that claims a tradition of centuries. The sense of timelessness is quite important. When the anthropologist asks the primitive why he performs a certain ritual, the answer might be, "because our ancestors have always done this." If in the modern-day United States our sense of tradition is a short one, we may find the same comfort in rituals realizing that we as individuals have always said the pledge or sung the hymn.

Comparatively speaking, the United States has never been overly enthusiastic about most rituals; many of our most important cultural values conflict with the values of ritual. Ritual celebrates permanence, while the U.S. values have stressed change; rituals celebrate the community while Americans extoll individualism and "going it alone." Ritual is rooted in the past; Americans are more concerned with the future. Nevertheless there has been a rise in the ritual function of communication for at least a sizable portion of the American public, particularly among the younger members. Indeed, part of what has come to be celebrated in some rituals might be considered as "youth," and yet another part of the ritual function has been to celebrate a youthful community as distinct from "the older generation," "the establishment," "the straight people," or whatever the outsiders happened to be called. In dress and hair styles, certainly in language and in music, in rallying figures (most notably among rock musicians), a kind of community was established. The "coming together" in marches, street protests, rock festivals like Woodstock, at religious revivals ("the Jesus freaks") was most remarkable. Apart from the apparent content of these events, which appears to be quite diverse, there is a common element which might best be described in terms of ritual satisfaction.

There appears to be little that is instrumental in the performance of a ritual, with some notable exceptions. Sociologist Robert Merton has noted that activities originally conceived as instrumental often become transmuted into ends in themselves. What was originally obtained through certain words or acts is no longer needed or desired. If at one time meat had to be prepared in a certain way to avoid contamination, meat may still be prepared in such a way because "that's the way our ancestors have always done it." If certain prayers were recited with the hope of rewards, the same prayers may be repeated even though a congregation no longer expects those rewards. In many, perhaps most, cases, a new mythology will develop to explain certain words and actions of a ritual. It is not clear whether rituals continue to exist by virtue of constant repetition or whether the participants in a ritual feel that some ends are being served.

Three characteristics of most rituals are most important: the rituals must be performed with others (immediately or symbolically present); they must be performed on some occasion; and they must be performed with special care to details.

This last characteristic makes ritual somewhat different from other forms of communication. Many children have difficulty with the high-level abstractions and archaic language often present in ritual. The usual vocabulary of children contains few high-level abstractions. But a child will learn to imitate or approximate the sounds of the rituals in which he finds himself participating. Frequently these words become translated in his own vocabulary without conflict. My niece and nephew, when very young, sang their favorite Christmas carol in church. The boy concluded "Silent Night" with the words "Sleep in heavenly beans." "No," his sister corrected, "not beans, peas."

Most of us have associations with aspects of some rituals from our earliest memories. Perhaps you have had the sudden awareness of what some words you have been saying all your life were really supposed to be. It can be both a startling and amusing realization. But it is one that characterizes a form of communication in which repetition of certain words over an expanse of time is most important.

For some persons, part of the appeal of ritual may be the pleasure of solemnly repeating words that seem to have no referent; this may evoke a mood of mystery for such persons. Other persons may find a deep satisfaction in discovering the meaning of what they have been saying for years. Such attitudes, if they exist, would seem to be unhealthy, not only as regards an understanding of the purpose of language but also for the significance of the ritual itself.

There are other characteristics of ritual that make it distinct from other functions of language in communication. One of these is the sublimation function of ritual. Through ritual, a person may symbolically take part in an event that would exclude his actual participation. During wartime, rituals tend to become more common and more significant. The displaying of the flag, the reciting of the pledge of allegiance, even the rationing of food and gasoline are ways of symbolically participating in the war effort. Or, to take a happier example, during a football game the fans who wish to help their team may better do so by cheering than by assisting on the field. It is common, for example, that at the kick-off the fans will go "sssssspoooom!" as if their noise will help to carry the ball farther down field.

Some rituals last longer than their mythologies. At a time when some persons begin to question religious beliefs, they may find it relatively easier to "lose the faith" than to lose the habit of prayer or church attendance on certain holy days. A sense of compulsiveness frequently attends ritual, and a sense of guilt may enter when ritual has gone. As a nation becomes what is called a "nontraditional society" the rituals that are a part of the tradition die. This finds expression as "alienation," the subject of many books, dramas, and films of recent years. It may also explain, in part, the current attraction for many philosophies of the "absurd." If a society's stability has been largely dependent on ritual and the rituals fall, it is an easy out to label the world as "absurd."

A final point should be made and emphasized. That is that what was intended for some purpose other than ritual can take on a ritual function. This may be a healthy addition to some other instrumental purpose, or it may be unhealthy if it substitutes for that other purpose. An example of the former might be the lasting effect of the Civil Rights March on Washington of 1963. No legislation was passed as a direct result of the march, but there was produced an important sense of community among white and Black that had not been exhibited so dramatically before.

Conventions of many kinds, political, social, and academic

many times serve more of a ritual function than the function of exchanging information or achieving some instrumental goal. To see the participants cheer or clap as the speaker speaks the holy jargon and drops the right names at the right time is amusing and a little sad at the same time. What is called a report may better serve as an incantation. No group can maintain itself without strong cohesiveness, it is true. But if the main result of the group's effort is only cohesiveness, then surely we have the origins of a new ritual.

On Saying What You Mean, and Meaning What You Say

Semanticists are sometimes thought to desire complete honesty of expression, directness, and "No beating around the bush." An understanding of the many purposes of communication should dispel that view. We use language for too many purposes and find ourselves forced to make some comment in too many difficult situations to hold to such a goal. Simple friendship, not to mention diplomacy and tact, prohibits us from always saying what we are thinking.

Suppose, for example, some friends are in a drama. You attend the opening-night performance, which is, as accurately as you can judge it, a real turkey. Then, as you leave the theater you encounter your friends and the director. Do you say what you are thinking and maybe hurt a friendship? Do you betray your critical integrity? No. Assuming that you cannot avoid comment, you equivocate, you speak in ambiguities. The popular expressions for this moment of untruth are many: (to the director): "Well, you've done it again!"; (to the actors): "You should have been in the audience!"; (to the elderly bystander who may be the dean, the director's father, or the playwright): "It was an unforgettable evening!"

If you feel that the potential ridicule of these expressions is too strong, you may equivocate further with the always safe "Congratulations!"

One may protest that these comments, however deft, are still lies and should not be excused. I think, however, that to so regard them is to confuse standards of different functions of communication.

Affective communication directed to the emotional responses of the listener does not require the accuracy, even of judgments, that the transmission of specific information does. The purpose is often friendship, not a critical evaluation. Often it is much more important to tell a person that you like his tie, coat, smile, voice, and so on, than to be bound by some standards of judgment which would severely limit your affective communications. A kind or friendly remark often does more for human understanding than a diplomatic silence or a hundred "honest" judgments.

To be aware of the many functions of communication is to be alive and sensitive to the most basic of human needs. As our needs for bodily health and comfort are met, we become more aware of (and create new) needs for symbolic health and comfort. To be loved or respected, to help others, to feel trust—the list could be elaborated greatly—becomes extremely important. Each communication situation both reveals our frailty and offers some promise for support.

SEVEN
AFTERWORD:
BEFORE LANGUAGE,
BEYOND LANGUAGE

Can a mature human being think without recourse to language? Can man ever transcend language to "something beyond" the limitations imposed by his language? As fascinating as these questions are, this is not the book in which to seek very satisfactory answers to them. We know that some meaningful acts can be performed without language, but we also know that little that is difficult or sophisticated can be achieved without the use of language in some form. The problem with these questions is that to date we seem to have no way of knowing the answers.

Reality and the Occult

Our discussion of man's thinking has been appropriate to the kind that is geared to man's physical and social reality. But there is also that vast and mysterious limbo of the less-than-conscious, the dream or hypnagogic state, which is not subject to reality-adjustment. After centuries of commentary by mystics and prophets, wise men and madmen, that reverie remains occult.

The very lack of information about what happens in this most personal kind of behavior might be taken as evidence that one may "experience" (if we may not say "think") before language, or, that one may go beyond language. The directional metaphor is probably irrelevant.

William James,[1] in his classic treatise on *The Varieties of Religious Experience*, observed that the most notable characteristic of mystics of all religions is the characteristic ineffability of their experiences:

> The handiest of the marks by which I classify a state of mind as mystical is negative. The subject of it immediately says that it defies expression, that no adequate report of its contents can be given in words. It follows from this that its quality must be directly experienced; it cannot be imparted or transferred to others.

We may conclude from this description that what the mystic has experienced has no use for words. Or, we may conclude that the difficulty is mostly one of translation from a personal language into a more general language. We simply do not know.

Persons under the influence of drugs report visions they cannot verbalize. This leads us to question whether the experiences are free from language entirely or whether the subject becomes especially critical of the reductive nature of language (an observation that should, of course, apply to *all* experiences). Aldous Huxley's[2] experience of looking at a vase of flowers while under the influence of mescaline is instructive:

> Fortuitous and provisional, the little nosegay broke all the rules of traditional good taste. At breakfast that morning I had been struck by the lively dissonance of its colors. But that was no longer the point. I was not looking now at an unusual flower arrangement. I was seeing what Adam had seen on the morning of his creation—the miracle, moment by moment, of naked existence.

[1] William James, *The Varieties of Religious Experience* (New York: Longmans, Green, and Co., 1902), p. 380.
[2] Aldous Huxley, *The Doors of Perception* (New York: Harper and Brothers, 1954), pp. 16, 17.

"Is it agreeable?" somebody asked. . . .

"Neither agreeable nor disagreeable," I answered. "It just is."

Huxley, it seems, was able to talk about an "it," but judgments about the "it" had no meaning. This irrelevance of categories for judgment or even for descriptions is also a common characteristic of the writings of mystics and prophets and, perhaps, some of the experiences of children. Only with the personal semantics of the adult aware of "his reality" do statements that go beyond describing sense impressions become important. Perhaps the average adult who comes closest to the one who says of an experience, "I would not go through it again, but neither would I trade that experience for any other." I have heard this said of the army, of love won and lost, of moments of terror and tragedy and achievement. The cliché seems to mean that although the judgment is positive (even for apparently disagreeable events), the judgment is limited to just *one* experience, and not that *kind* of experience. The distinction is most important.

If there is a street corner in Heaven where the souls gather to reminisce about Life, surely this same cliché is often repeated: "I would not go through it again, but neither would I trade that experience for any other." (Not that we have any choice, of course.) At the time of an experience, be it pain, fear, love, or life, the most sensitive person can only *experience*, without judgment and even without verbalization.

Most of us, however, go through life attempting to endow each experience with meaning, to make sense of our sensing. As minor poets, historians, and scientists—all of us—we try to tell ourselves and others where to stand and how to look in order to duplicate experiences. We feel we can comprehend only the familiar and we know that we can communicate only the familiar.

But experience can never be communicated. The meaning we "discover" in our experiences is the meaning we put there. Each man *is* the measure of all things, and his own judgments, his own descriptions, and all the resources of his language cannot duplicate that experience for another person or even for himself. Once an event is experienced it alters all subsequent experiences. Once an event is verbalized, it is no longer *that* event.

Thus we come full circle. We return to the kind of pure sense data that is not "this or that," but *just is*. It was this that Northrop[3] observed in the logic of the sciences: "The pure empiricists are the mystics of the world, as the Orientals, who have tended to restrict knowledge to the immediately experienced. . . . Pure fact is a continuum of ineffable aesthetic qualities. . . ."

When we understand language and communication we may better know how to communicate what we *can* express. This is the lesson of semantics. But, also, when we understand language and communication we know that we can never communicate all that we may *wish* to express. Meaning is a personal thing. This, too, is the lesson of semantics.

[3] F. S. C. Northrop, *The Logic of the Sciences and the Humanities* (New York: World Publishing Co., 1959, by arrangement with Macmillan), pp. 40–41.

RECOMMENDED
READING

Allport, Floyd H. *Theories of Perception and the Concept of Structure*. New York: John Wiley and Sons, 1955.

Barnlund, Dean C. *Interpersonal Communication: Survey and Studies*. Boston: Houghton Mifflin, 1969.

Berger, Peter and Thomas Luckman. *The Social Construction of Reality*. Garden City: Doubleday Anchor, 1966.

Berlo, David. *The Process of Communication*. New York: Holt, Rinehart and Winston, 1960.

Birdwhistell, Ray L. *Kinesics and Context*. Philadelphia: Univ. of Pennsylvania Press, 1971.

Boas, Franz. *The Mind of Primitive Man*. New York: Macmillan, 1938.

Bois, Samuel. *Explorations in Awareness*. New York: Harper & Row, 1957.

Bronowski, J. *Science and Human Values*. Baltimore: Penguin Books, 1964.

Brown, Roger. *Words and Things*. Glencoe: The Free Press, 1958.

Burke, Kenneth. *A Grammar of Motives*. New York: Prentice-Hall, 1955.

———. *A Philosophy of Literary Form*. New York: Prentice-Hall, 1941.

Carroll, John. *The Study of Language*. Cambridge: Harvard Univ. Press, 1953.

Cassirer, Ernst. *Language and Myth*. New York: Harper & Row, 1946

Chase, Stuart. *The Power of Words*. New York: Harcourt Brace Jovanovich, 1954.

Condon, John. *A Bibliography of General Semantics*. (Originally published by *ETC.: A Review of General Semantics* in five installments; available from the International Society for General Semantics.)

————and Fathi Yousef. *Intercultural Communication*. Indianapolis: Bobbs-Merrill, 1974.

ETC.: A Review of General Semantics. (published quarterly)

Goodstein, R. L., "Language and Experience," in Arthur Danto and Sidney Morgenbesser (eds.) *Philosophy of Science*. New York: World Publishing Co., 1959, p. 1–132.

Gorman, Margaret. *The Educational Implications of the Theory of Meaning and Symbolism of General Semantics*. Washington, D.C.: The Catholic Univ. of America Press, 1958.

Hall, Edward T. *The Silent Language*. New York: Doubleday, 1959.

Hastorf, Albert H. and Hadley Cantril, "They Saw a Game: A Case Study," *The Journal of Abnormal and Social Psychology* 49 (January, 1954) (Reprinted as Bobbs-Merrill Reprint in the Social Sciences, Number P–147.)

Hayakawa, S. I. (ed.) *Language, Meaning and Maturity*. New York: Harper & Row, 1954.

————. *Language in Thought and Action*, Second Edition. New York: Harcourt Brace Jovanovich, 1964.

————(ed.) *Our Language and Our World*. New York: Harper & Row, 1959.

————. *Symbol, Status, and Personality*. New York: Harcourt Brace Jovanovich, 1963.

————(ed.) *The Use and Misuse of Language*. New York: Fawcett, 1962.

Heinlein, Robert. *A Stranger in a Strange Land*. Berkeley: Berkeley Medallian Books, 1961. (A science fiction novel.)

Henle, Paul (ed.). *Language, Thought and Culture*. Ann Arbor: Ann Arbor Paperbacks, 1965.

Holton, Gerald (ed.) *Science and Culture*. Boston: Beacon Press, 1967.

Johnson, Wendell. *Your Most Enchanted Listener*. New York: Harper & Row, 1956.

Korzybski, Alfred. *Science and Sanity: An Introduction to Non-Aristotelian Systems and General Semantics*. Lancaster, Penn.: Science Press Printing Co., 1933.

――――. *Selections from Science and Sanity*. Compiled and arranged by Guthrie Janssen. Lakeville, Conn.: Institute of General Semantics, 1947.

Langer, Susanne K. *Philosophy in a New Key*. Cambridge: Harvard Univ. Press, 1942.

Lee, Dorothy. *Freedom and Culture*. Englewood Cliffs, N.J.: Prentice-Hall, 1959.

Lee, Irving. *Customs and Crises in Communication*. New York: Harper & Row, 1954.

――――. *The Language of Wisdom and Folly*. New York: Harper & Row, 1949.

Lenneberg, Eric. *The Biological Foundations of Language*. New York: John Wiley and Sons, 1967.

McKellar, Peter. *Imagination and Thinking: A Psychological Analysis*. New York: Basic Books, 1957.

Melleson, Andrew. *The Medical Runaround*. New York: Hart, 1974.

Miller, George. *Language and Communication*. New York: McGraw-Hill, 1951.

Morris, Charles. *Signs, Language and Behavior*. Englewood Cliffs, N.J.: Prentice-Hall, 1946.

Northrop, F. S. C. *The Logic of the Sciences and the Humanities*. New York: Macmillan, 1947.

Ogden, C. K. and I. A. Richards. *The Meaning of Meaning*, Third Edition Revised. New York: Harcourt Brace Jovanovich, 1930.

Orwell, George. *1984*. London: George Allen, 1948.

Osgood, Charles, George J. Suci, and Percy H. Tannenbaum. *The Measurement of Meaning*. Urbana: University of Illinois Press, 1957.

Piaget, Jean. *The Language and Thought of the Child*. New York: Harcourt Brace Jovanovich, 1926.

Popper, Karl R. *The Logic of Scientific Discovery*. New York: Science Editions, 1961.

Rapoport, Anatol. *Fights, Games and Debates*. New York: Harper & Row, 1960.

――――. *Operational Philosophy*. New York: Harper & Row, 1953.

Reichenbach, Hans. *The Rise of Scientific Philosophy*. Berkeley: University of California Press, 1959.

Rogers, Carl R. *On Becoming a Person*. Boston: Houghton Mifflin, 1967.

Ruesch, Jurgen. *Therapeutic Communication*. New York: W. W. Norton, 1961.

———and Gregory Bateson. *Communication: The Social Matrix of Psychiatry*. New York: W. W. Norton, 1951.

Russell, Bertrand. *An Inquiry into Meaning and Truth*. Baltimore: Penguin Books, 1962.

Sapir, Edward. *Language: An Introduction to the Study of Speech*. New York: Harcourt Brace Jovanovich, 1921.

Saporta, Sol (ed.) *Psycholinguistics: A Book of Readings*. New York: Holt, Rinehart and Winston, 1961.

Satir, Virginia. *Conjoint Family Therapy*. Palo Alto: Science Books, 1964.

Shannon, Clyde and Warren Weaver. *The Mathematical Theory of Communication*. Urbana: University of Illinois Press, 1951.

Stewart, Edward C. *American Cultural Patterns: A Cross-Cultural Perspective*. Pittsburgh: Regional Council for International Education, 1971.

Ullmann, Stephen. *Semantics: An Introduction to the Science of Meaning*. New York: Barnes and Noble, 1962.

Von Bertalanffy, Ludwig. *General Systems Theory*. New York: Braziller, 1968.

Watzlawick, Paul, Janet Beavin, and Don Jackson. *The Pragmatics of Human Communication*. New York: W. W. Norton, 1967.

Weinberg, Harry. *Levels of Knowing and Existence*. New York: Harper & Row, 1959.

White, Leslie. *The Science of Culture*. New York: Grove Press, 1963.

Whorf, Benjamin Lee. *Language, Thought and Reality: Selected Writings of Benjamin Lee Whorf* (John B. Carroll, ed.) New York: John Wiley and Sons, 1956.

Wiener, Norbert. *The Human Use of Human Beings: Cybernetics and Society*. Boston: Houghton Mifflin, 1950.

INDEX

COMMUNICATION

SECOND EDITION

MACMILLAN PUBLISHING CO., INC.
New York

COLLIER MACMILLAN PUBLISHERS
London

P90
C64
1975

Macmillan Publishing Co., Inc.
866 Third Avenue, New York, New York 10022

Collier-Macmillan Canada, Ltd.

Library of Congress Cataloging in Publication Data

Condon, John C
  Semantics and communication.

  Bibliography: p.
  1. Communication. 2. Interpersonal relations.
3. English language—Semantics. I. Title.
P90.C64   1975   422   74-3800
ISBN 0-02-324220-5

Printing: 1 2 3 4 5 6 7 8   Year: 5 6 7 8 9 0